Strength and Strategy

Strength and Strategy

ASSESSING GULF ARMIES' EFFICIENCY ON THE FIELD.

GEW Intelligence Unit

HICHEM KAROUI (ED.)

Global East-West (London)

Copyright © 2024 by GEW Intelligence Unit

All rights reserved. No part of this book may be reproduced in any manner whatsoever without written permission except in the case of brief quotations embodied in critical articles and reviews.

First Printing, 2024

Contents

I	Introduction	1
II	Military Spending and Modernization	13
	Sources and References	25
III	Operational Challenges and Ineffectiveness	27
	Sources and References	41
IV	Comparative Military Strength	43
	Sources and References	54
V	Internal and External Security Challenges	56
	Sources and References	72
VI	Evaluating Training and Personnel	74
	Sources and References	85
VII	Utilization of Technology and Innovation	87
	Sources and References	103
VIII	Regional Alliances and Partnerships	105
	Sources and references	119
IX	Crisis Management and Conflict Resolution	121
	Sources and references	133
X	Future Prospects and Recommendations	135

1

Introduction

Military Investment Trends in the Gulf States

The Gulf states' strategic imperative to invest substantially in defense and security capabilities stems from a complex regional landscape characterized by geopolitical rivalries, militant threats, and ongoing conflicts. As a pivotal player in the Gulf Cooperation Council (GCC), Saudi Arabia has historically maintained a robust defense posture, driven by its leadership role in regional security dynamics and as a key ally of Western powers. The Kingdom's defense spending has not only enabled it to acquire advanced military hardware but also facilitated the development of local defense industries through strategic partnerships with global defense manufacturers and technology transfer agreements.

The United Arab Emirates (UAE) stands out for its rapid ascent as a regional military power, leveraging its significant financial resources to procure cutting-edge military equipment and enhance its defense capabilities. The UAE's unique emphasis on innovation and technology in defense manufacturing reflects its ambition to establish a sustainable defense industrial base and reduce reliance on foreign suppliers. Qatar, while emerging as a key defense spender in the region, has prioritized acquiring a diverse range of military assets to address specific security challenges and project influence beyond its borders.

The evolving security dynamics in the Gulf, compounded by the rise of non-state actors, cyber threats, and unconventional warfare tactics, have necessitated a holistic approach to defense investment and modernization. Traditional military threats do not solely drive the Gulf states' pursuit of military modernization but also encompasses readiness to counter asymmetric threats, protect critical infrastructure, and address emerging security domains such as space and cyberspace. Strengthening defense resilience through advanced technologies, intelligence capabilities, and integrated command and control systems remains a strategic imperative for Gulf armies to effectively adapt to dynamic security challenges.

Operational Efficiency and Effectiveness Challenges

Despite the significant strides made in modernizing their armed forces, the Gulf states face persistent challenges in optimizing operational efficiency and readiness. While providing access to cutting-edge technologies, the reliance on imported military equipment often leads to logistical complexities, maintenance issues, and compatibility challenges with existing platforms. Moreover, some Gulf armed forces have identified gaps in operational readiness and training deficiencies, highlighting the need for continuous capacity-building efforts and professional development initiatives.

Enhancing coordination and interoperability among Gulf armies remains a critical challenge due to variations in military doctrines, operational procedures, and language barriers. Strengthening joint training exercises, interoperability mechanisms, and information-sharing platforms can foster greater military integration and interoperability among Gulf forces, enhancing their collective effectiveness in responding to regional security threats. Addressing human capital challenges, including enhancing leadership skills, promoting a culture of innovation, and investing in specialized training programs, is essential to building a professional and proficient military workforce capable of meeting evolving security demands.

Comparative Military Strength and Regional Dynamics

The comparative military strength of Gulf states, shaped by their defense investments, military capabilities, and regional security partnerships, is pivotal in influencing power dynamics and shaping regional security architectures. With their advanced military arsenals and expeditionary capabilities, Saudi Arabia and the UAE have increasingly assumed roles as regional security providers, engaging in coalition operations, counterterrorism missions, and maritime security patrols to safeguard shared interests in the Gulf region and beyond.

Egypt, a heavyweight in the Arab world with a strong military tradition, maintains strategic security alliances with Gulf states to address common security challenges and promote regional stability. Iran's expanding military influence, characterized by its paramilitary proxies and ballistic missile arsenal, poses a complex security challenge to Gulf states, compelling them to augment their defense capabilities and strengthen security cooperation initiatives. The ongoing conflicts in Yemen, Syria, and Iraq underscore the volatile security environment in the Gulf region, necessitating sustained military preparedness, cooperation, and resilience among Gulf armies to mitigate security risks effectively and uphold regional stability.

A. BACKGROUND ON GULF STATES' MILITARY INVESTMENTS

Gulf states have a long history of significant military investments, dating back to the post-independence era when these countries sought to establish strong, capable armed forces to safeguard their newly acquired sovereignty. The strategic location of the Gulf region, at the crossroads of major trade routes and in proximity to critical energy resources, has always made it a hotspot for international interests and potential conflicts.

The concept of militarization in the Gulf can be traced back to the early 20th century, with the establishment of the Trucial States – precursor states to the United Arab Emirates – and their reliance on British security arrangements for protection against external threats. This colonial legacy laid the foundation for the subsequent development of local military forces in the region, as Gulf rulers sought to assert their autonomy and enhance their ability to defend against potential adversaries.

The advent of the Cold War in the mid-20th century further heightened the security concerns of Gulf states, as they were caught in the crossfire of superpower competition and ideological rivalries. The Eisenhower Doctrine of 1957, which aimed to contain the spread of communism in the Middle East, led to increased U.S. military presence and assistance to Gulf countries, further reinforcing their strategic importance in the global balance of power.

The Iranian Revolution of 1979 and the subsequent Iran-Iraq War (1980-1988) represented another turning point in the militarization of the Gulf. As neighboring states grappled with the destabilizing effects of regional conflict and the specter of revolutionary movements inspired by Ayatollah Khomeini's radical ideology, Gulf states responded by investing heavily in their armed forces, acquiring advanced weaponry, and forging alliances with Western powers to bolster their defenses against potential Iranian threats.

The Gulf War in 1990-91, triggered by Iraq's invasion of Kuwait, was a seismic event that exposed the vulnerabilities of Gulf states and underscored the imperative of collective security arrangements to deter aggression and preserve regional stability. The formation of the Gulf Cooperation Council (GCC) in 1981 and the subsequent establishment of the Peninsula Shield Force as a joint defense mechanism reflected a newfound sense of unity and common purpose among Gulf countries in confronting external challenges.

Furthermore, the emergence of transnational terrorist organizations such as Al-Qaeda, ISIS, and others has posed a multifaceted security dilemma for Gulf states, necessitating a comprehensive approach to counter-terrorism that encompasses military, intelligence, law enforcement, and ideological dimensions. Hybrid warfare, characterized by the blending of conventional and irregular tactics in an increasingly interconnected and information-driven world, has raised new challenges for Gulf states in defending their borders, critical infrastructure, and societal resilience against asymmetric threats.

In conclusion, the militarization of the Gulf region is a complex and multifaceted process shaped by a confluence of historical, geopolitical, and security factors. By examining the evolution of military investments in the Gulf through a historical lens, one can gain a deeper appreciation of the strategic imperatives, threats, and opportunities that have driven the defense policies of these countries and continue to influence their approach to national security in an uncertain and rapidly changing global environment.

B. IMPORTANCE OF ASSESSING GULF ARMIES' EFFICIENCY

Background on Gulf states' military investments is crucial for understanding the region's security landscape and potential vulnerabilities. As Gulf states continue to allocate significant resources to their defense sectors, it becomes essential to assess the efficiency of their armies to determine their readiness and capabilities in responding to various security challenges.

An in-depth analysis of the efficiency of Gulf armies involves examining multiple facets of their military structures. This includes evaluating the size and composition of their forces, the level of training and preparedness of their personnel, the quality and quantity of their equipment and weaponry, and their ability to collaborate effectively with international partners. Assessing these factors provides a comprehensive understanding of the overall strength and resilience of Gulf armies in the face of diverse threats.

Gulf states have made substantial investments in modernizing their defense capabilities in recent years, acquiring state-of-the-art military equipment and technologies to enhance their operational effectiveness. From advanced fighter jets like the F-35 Lightning II and Eurofighter Typhoon to naval vessels equipped with missile defence systems such as Aegis Combat System, these investments demonstrate a commitment to maintaining a credible deterrence posture and bolstering their defence capabilities against a wide range of security challenges.

The efficiency of Gulf armies is also reflected in their ability to conduct joint military exercises and operations. Collaborative efforts among Gulf states and their strategic partners demonstrate a commitment to interoperability, coordination, and shared security objectives. Notable joint exercises include the biennial "Gulf Shield" drills, which bring together military forces from Gulf Cooperation Council (GCC) countries to enhance their readiness and coordination in responding to regional security threats.

Furthermore, assessing the efficiency of Gulf armies involves evaluating their command and control structures, intelligence capabilities, and defense industrial base. Effective command and control mechanisms ensure timely decision-making and coordinated responses during crises. Intelligence capabilities, including surveillance and reconnaissance assets, are vital in gathering actionable intelligence and maintaining situational awareness to preempt potential threats.

In addition, developing a robust defense industrial base is crucial for enhancing self-reliance and reducing dependency on foreign suppliers for critical defense equipment and technologies. Gulf states have increasingly focused on building local defence manufacturing capabilities to support their military modernization efforts and promote technological innovation within their defense industries.

Moreover, Gulf armies' efficiency is also dependent on their logistical capabilities and sustainment processes. Adequate logistical support, efficient supply chains, and robust infrastructure are essential for ensuring military forces' readiness and operational effectiveness. By investing in modern logistics systems and infrastructure projects, Gulf states can enhance their military mobility, agility, and responsiveness to emerging security challenges.

In conclusion, a comprehensive assessment of Gulf armies' efficiency is essential for strategic planning, risk management, and capability development. By delving into the various dimensions of their military capabilities, Gulf states can better position themselves to address evolving security threats, enhance regional stability, and effectively respond to complex security challenges in a rapidly changing global environment.

C. OVERVIEW OF KEY DIMENSIONS EXAMINED IN THE BOOK

This section examines the main factors explored in the book about the effectiveness of Gulf armies. It looks closely at each factor to give a complete picture of the complex issues and challenges that military forces in the Gulf encounter.

1. Military Spending and Modernization:

The historical military spending trends in Gulf states reveal a consistent pattern of substantial investments in modernization efforts. Gulf countries prioritize acquiring advanced weapons systems and defense capabilities to enhance their military readiness and power projection capabilities. The emphasis on modernization reflects the strategic imperative of keeping pace with evolving security threats and maintaining a credible deterrent posture in the region. Gulf states' reliance on external support, particularly from

Western allies, underscores the collaborative nature of defense procurement and technology transfer agreements bolstering their military capabilities.

2. Operational Challenges and Ineffectiveness:

Institutional weaknesses within Gulf militaries present significant operational challenges, ranging from deficiencies in decision-making processes to shortcomings in command structures and coordination among different branches of the armed forces. These challenges hinder operational effectiveness and complex operational environments, where agility, interoperability, and situational awareness are critical for mission success. Gulf militaries must address these institutional gaps through reforms, training programs, and joint exercises to enhance their combat readiness and operational efficiency in the face of diverse security threats and evolving warfare dynamics.

3. Comparative Military Strength:

Various indices used to rank military powers in the Middle East provide insights into the relative capabilities of Gulf states compared to regional powers like Iran and Israel. The comprehensive analysis of military strength considers factors such as personnel size, weapon systems inventory, defense spending, and operational readiness to gauge the relative power balance in the region. Gulf states' investments in defense modernization, training programs, and strategic partnerships influence their standing in comparative military rankings, shaping regional dynamics and security perceptions among key stakeholders.

4. Internal and External Security Challenges:

Internal security threats, including domestic unrest, terrorism, and sectarian tensions, test the resilience of Gulf states' security apparatus and expose vulnerabilities that can impact military effectiveness. Governance uncertainties and socioeconomic disparities contribute to internal security challenges that require holistic approaches to address root causes and mitigate risks to stability. External security challenges, such as regional rivalries, maritime security threats, and proxy conflicts, necessitate a strategic recalibration of Gulf states' defense posture to navigate complex security environments and safeguard national interests in a volatile geopolitical landscape.

5. Evaluating Training and Personnel:

The quality of military personnel and the effectiveness of training programs play crucial roles in enhancing Gulf military capabilities and operational effectiveness. Investments in professional development, leadership training, and specialized skill sets are essential to cultivating a highly competent and adaptable force capable of meeting the evolving demands of modern warfare. Gulf states must prioritize continuous training, simulation exercises, and knowledge sharing to elevate the proficiency and resilience of their military personnel, ensuring they are well-prepared to address a diverse array of security challenges and operational scenarios.

6. Utilization of Technology and Innovation:

Integrating cutting-edge technologies and innovative solutions into Gulf militaries' operational capabilities signifies a strategic shift towards leveraging technological advancements to enhance military effectiveness and efficiency. From unmanned aerial vehicles (UAVs) and cyber warfare capabilities to artificial intelligence and satellite communications systems, Gulf states invest in diverse technological platforms to augment their combat capabilities and information superiority. Adopting advanced technologies presents opportunities to enhance situational awareness, accelerate decision-making processes, and maximise operational outcomes in dynamic and competitive security environments.

7. Regional Alliances and Partnerships:

Gulf states' military alliances and partnerships are instrumental in promoting collective security, interoperability, and shared defense responsibilities among regional stakeholders. Collaborative initiatives within the Gulf Cooperation Council (GCC), bilateral defense agreements, and joint military exercises with Western allies strengthen Gulf states' defense capabilities and crisis response mechanisms. Enhanced regional cooperation fosters trust, information sharing, and burden-sharing among allied nations, bolstering deterrence capabilities and promoting regional stability in the face of common security challenges.

8. Crisis Management and Conflict Resolution:

Effective crisis management within Gulf armies requires a multi-faceted approach encompassing rapid response mechanisms, contingency planning, and crisis communication strategies to mitigate security risks and prevent conflicts from escalating. The ability to navigate complex security crises, including asymmetric threats, hybrid warfare tactics, and geopolitical tensions, necessitates agile decision-making, interagency coordination, and strategic foresight within Gulf military institutions. Lessons learned from past conflicts and peacekeeping operations inform best practices for conflict resolution, mediation efforts, and humanitarian assistance initiatives to promote regional security and stability in the Gulf region.

By delving deep into these key dimensions, this chapter offers a comprehensive analysis of the intricate factors influencing Gulf armies' operational efficiency and military effectiveness. It illuminates the nuanced challenges, strategic imperatives, and collaborative opportunities that shape the security landscape of the Gulf region, providing readers with a holistic perspective on the evolving dynamics of Gulf military capabilities and their implications for regional security architecture.

Military Spending and Modernization

Defense Diplomacy and Strategic Partnerships

In addition to military modernization efforts, Gulf states have actively engaged in defense diplomacy and forged strategic partnerships with key international allies to enhance their security cooperation and address regional security challenges. The Gulf Cooperation Council (GCC) is a platform for member states to collaborate on defense and security issues, enabling them to undertake joint military exercises, intelligence sharing, and coordinated responses to common threats. Furthermore, Gulf countries have developed close defense ties with major powers such as the United States, the United Kingdom, France, and Russia, providing them with advanced military equipment, training, and logistical support to bolster their defense capabilities.

Human Capital Development and Military Training

Gulf states have prioritized investments in human capital development and military training to enhance their armed forces' professional skills and operational readiness. Military personnel are offered high-quality education and training programs to ensure they are equipped with the necessary expertise to operate advanced defense technologies effectively. Specialized cybersecurity, counter-terrorism, and special operations training has become crucial in preparing Gulf forces to address modern security threats. Additionally, military exchanges, joint exercises with international partners, and participation in peacekeeping missions have enhanced interoperability and built strategic relationships with allied nations.

Defense Industry Growth and Economic Diversification

The growth of the defense industry in the Gulf region has been driven by efforts to diversify national economies, create job opportunities, and reduce reliance on oil revenues. Gulf countries have established defense industrial bases and technological hubs to facilitate the development of local defense capabilities and support the local manufacturing of military equipment. Initiatives to promote defense research and innovation, establish defense research institutes, and provide incentives for private sector participation in defense production have contributed to the growth of a robust defense industry ecosystem in the region. Furthermore, defense exports have emerged as a key component of economic diversification strategies, with Gulf states seeking to position themselves as global defense exporters and contribute to the growth of the defense sector on a regional and international scale.

Ethical and Legal Considerations in Military Spending

As Gulf states continue to expand their defense budgets and invest in military modernization, ethical and legal considerations have become increasingly important in shaping defense policies and decision-making processes. Transparency, accountability, and adherence to international norms and standards are essential principles that guide military spending and procurement practices in the Gulf region. Measures to combat corruption, ensure compliance with arms control treaties, and uphold humanitarian law in armed conflicts are paramount to maintaining the integrity of defense investments and promoting responsible defense governance. Moreover, efforts to enhance civilian oversight of defense expenditure, establish mechanisms for public disclosure of defense budgets, and engage civil society organizations in defense policy discussions are vital steps in promoting good governance and fostering public trust in defense institutions.

Conclusion

In conclusion, the dynamics of military spending in the Gulf region are influenced by a complex interplay of political, security, economic, and technological factors that shape the defense priorities and strategies of Gulf states. The sustained focus on military modernization, technological innovation, defense diplomacy, human capital development, and ethical considerations underscores the multifaceted nature of defense investment in the region. As Gulf states navigate the evolving security landscape and confront emerging challenges, they must continue balancing their defense requirements with broader national interests, fostering strategic partnerships, promoting transparency and accountability, and upholding ethical standards to ensure the long-term sustainability and effectiveness of their defense policies and capabilities.

A. OVERVIEW OF GULF STATES' MILITARY SPENDING TRENDS

In recent years, the Gulf states have indeed undergone a significant transformation in their military capabilities, characterized by a comprehensive modernization drive that has reshaped the regional security landscape. This overhaul of defense postures and procurement strategies has been influenced by many factors, including geopolitical shifts, evolving security threats, and domestic imperatives for economic diversification and industrial development.

Saudi Arabia, as the largest and most influential Gulf state, has emerged as a critical player in shaping the regional military dynamics. With a combination of substantial financial resources and strategic partnerships with major global defense suppliers, the Kingdom has embarked on ambitious military modernization programs aimed at enhancing its operational capabilities across land, air, and sea domains. Investments in state-of-the-art fighter jets, ballistic missile defense systems, and naval assets have not only bolstered Saudi Arabia's defense capabilities but also elevated its status as a power projection actor in the broader Middle East.

The United Arab Emirates (UAE), another prominent player in the Gulf, has pursued a similar trajectory of military modernization with a distinct emphasis on building a robust local defense industry. Through strategic alliances and joint ventures with international defense contractors, the UAE has made significant strides in developing advanced military technologies and enhancing its self-sufficiency in defense production. This strategic approach not only enhances the UAE's military capabilities but also spurs economic growth and technological innovation in the country.

Qatar, despite its relatively smaller size compared to its neighbors, has demonstrated a strong commitment to bolstering its defense capabilities through strategic acquisitions and investments. The country's procurement of cutting-edge fighter jets, air defense systems, and maritime assets reflects its strategic ambitions to fortify its security posture and assert its regional influence. Additionally, Qatar's proactive efforts in fostering international defense partnerships and participating in multilateral security initiatives have further cemented its role as a key security actor in the Gulf region.

Moreover, the Gulf states' increasing focus on cybersecurity and information warfare highlights their recognition of the evolving nature of security threats in the digital age. As cyber warfare capabilities become integral to modern defense strategies, Gulf countries have stepped up efforts to enhance their cyber defenses, intelligence capabilities, and electronic warfare systems to safeguard their critical infrastructure and mitigate cyber threats. This proactive approach strengthens their ability to defend against cyber attacks and underscores their commitment to staying ahead of emerging security challenges in an interconnected world.

In conclusion, the Gulf states' comprehensive modernization of their military capabilities signifies a strategic shift towards enhancing their defense readiness, projecting power regionally, and adapting to emerging security paradigms. By investing in advanced weaponry, fostering local defense industries, and prioritizing cybersecurity, the Gulf countries are actively preparing themselves to meet the complex security challenges of the 21st century and assert their influence on the global stage.

B. ANALYSIS OF INVESTMENTS IN ADVANCED WEAPONS SYSTEMS AND DEFENSE INFRASTRUCTURE

Gulf states have invested significantly in advanced weapons systems and defense infrastructure to enhance their military capabilities and protect national security interests. These investments are a response to the changing security landscape in the region, characterized by ongoing conflicts, geopolitical tensions, and the proliferation of advanced military technologies. By acquiring cutting-edge weaponry, Gulf states aim to bolster their defense capabilities, project power regionally, and maintain a credible deterrence posture against potential adversaries.

One of the key areas of investment has been in air defense systems, with Gulf states acquiring sophisticated missile defense systems to protect their territories from airborne threats. Patriot batteries and THAAD (Terminal High Altitude Area Defense) systems have been procured to intercept and destroy incoming missiles, providing a layered defense against ballistic missile attacks. This multi-layered approach not only enhances the overall defense capabilities but also increases the survivability of critical assets in the event of a missile strike. Furthermore, Gulf states have also invested in radar systems, such as the AN/TPY-2 radar, which enhances their ability to detect and track incoming threats, providing early warning and timely response actions.

In the realm of air superiority, Gulf states have made substantial investments in acquiring advanced fighter jets with advanced avionics, stealth capabilities, and precision strike capabilities. These advanced platforms, such as the F-16, F-35, and Eurofighter Typhoon, provide Gulf states with a significant edge in aerial combat scenarios and enable them to project power both defensively and offensively. Additionally, integrating these fighter jets with air-to-air missiles and stand-off weapons further enhances the operational effectiveness of Gulf state air forces, allowing them to engage and neutralize threats with precision and speed.

In the naval domain, Gulf states have expanded their naval capabilities by acquiring modern warships equipped with state-of-the-art weapons systems and sensors. Adding frigates, corvettes, and fast attack craft to their fleets enhances their maritime presence. It enables them to conduct various maritime operations, from coastal defense to anti-surface and anti-submarine warfare. These naval assets also contribute to safeguarding vital maritime trade routes, ensuring the security of sea lanes critical for global commerce and energy transportation. Moreover, Gulf states have invested in marine patrol aircraft, unmanned maritime systems, and naval helicopters to enhance their maritime surveillance capabilities and extend their reach in monitoring and securing their maritime borders.

In parallel to weapons acquisitions, Gulf states have focused on developing robust defense infrastructure, including command and control centers, secure communication networks, and training facilities. These infrastructure investments aim to improve the efficiency and effectiveness of military operations, ensuring seamless coordination and information sharing among different branches of the armed forces. Furthermore, investments in cybersecurity capabilities and resilience technologies are essential to safeguarding Gulf states' defense networks from cyber threats and ensuring the integrity and confidentiality of sensitive military information.

Overall, the strategic investments in advanced weapons systems and defense infrastructure underscore Gulf states' commitment to enhancing their military capabilities and safeguarding their national security interests in a complex and volatile regional environment. As Gulf states continue to modernize their armed forces and adapt to evolving security challenges, the effective utilization and integration of advanced technologies will be crucial in maintaining deterrence, countering threats, and promoting stability in the region for the foreseeable future.

C. EXAMINATION OF RELIANCE ON EXTERNAL SUPPORT, PARTICULARLY FROM THE UNITED STATES

Gulf states have historically relied on external support, particularly from the United States, to augment their military capabilities and enhance their national security posture. This reliance dates back to the Cold War era when the U.S. sought to build a network of alliances in the Middle East to counter Soviet influence and safeguard its strategic interests in the region. The Gulf states, in turn, viewed the United States as a key ally and provider of security guarantees in a volatile and tumultuous regional environment.

One significant aspect of the Gulf states' reliance on external support is acquiring advanced military equipment and technology from the United States. Over the years, Gulf countries have invested billions of dollars in procuring sophisticated weapons systems, including fighter jets, missile defense systems, and naval vessels, from American defense contractors. This infusion of cutting-edge weaponry has not only bolstered the Gulf states' defense capabilities but also served as a force multiplier in deterring potential adversaries and maintaining a credible defense posture.

Moreover, the Gulf states have benefited from U.S. military training programs, advisory missions, and joint exercises that have enhanced their military readiness and operational effectiveness. The close collaboration between the Gulf countries and the U.S. military has fostered interoperability, information sharing, and strategic coordination, contributing to regional security and stability.

However, this reliance on external support, particularly from the United States, has raised concerns about the sustainability of Gulf states' defense capabilities and the potential risks of overreliance on a single security partner. In recent years, geopolitical shifts, changing U.S. foreign policy priorities, and regional dynamics have prompted Gulf countries to reassess their strategic dependencies and explore avenues for diversification.

To mitigate their vulnerability to fluctuations in external support, Gulf states are increasingly investing in building localdefense industries and capabilities. By developing domestic defense production capabilities, Gulf countries aim to reduce their reliance on foreign suppliers, enhance technological self-sufficiency, and ensure continuity in defense procurement efforts.

Furthermore, Gulf states are actively pursuing strategic partnerships with other global powers, such as China, Russia, and European countries, to diversify their security relationships and reduce their dependence on any single ally. Through joint military exercises, defense cooperation agreements, and technology transfer initiatives, Gulf countries seek to expand their strategic options and hedge against potential disruptions in their traditional security alliances.

In navigating the complex interplay of external support and national security imperatives, Gulf states face a delicate balancing act between leveraging the benefits of international partnerships and preserving their autonomy and strategic independence. The evolving security landscape in the Middle East underscores the importance of strategic foresight, innovation, and adaptability as Gulf countries navigate the challenges of maintaining their security posture in a rapidly changing geopolitical environment.

As Gulf states continue to navigate the intricacies of their external relationships and security partnerships, they must also factor in the evolving dynamics of regional conflicts, shifting power structures, and emerging threats. The rise of non-state actors, cyber warfare capabilities, and asymmetrical threats present new challenges that require innovative approaches and adaptive strategies.

Additionally, the Gulf states are increasingly focused on enhancing their counterterrorism capabilities, maritime security measures, and disaster response protocols to address evolving security threats in the region. By investing in advanced surveillance systems, intelligence-sharing mechanisms, and joint maritime patrols, Gulf countries are working to strengthen their collective security architecture and fortify their defenses against a range of potential security challenges.

Moreover, the Gulf states are exploring opportunities for multilateral security cooperation and information-sharing platforms to enhance their collective resilience and response capabilities in the face of complex security threats. By fostering closer ties with regional organizations, such as the Gulf Cooperation Council (GCC) and the Arab League, Gulf countries seek to leverage collective resources, expertise, and operational coordination to address shared security concerns and promote regional stability.

In conclusion, the Gulf states' reliance on external support, particularly from the United States, remains critical to their national security strategies. However, in light of evolving geopolitical dynamics and strategic imperatives, Gulf countries actively pursue a diversified approach to enhancing their defense capabilities, strengthening their partnerships, and securing their national interests in an increasingly complex and uncertain security environment.

IN A NUTSHELL

Overview of Gulf States' Military Spending Trends

The Gulf states have exhibited significant increases in military spending, driven by geopolitical tensions and the need to modernize their armed forces. In 2023, Middle East countries, including Gulf states, spent 4.2% of their GDP on defense, the highest rate globally. Saudi Arabia and Qatar, in particular, have seen sharp increases in their military expenditures. Saudi Arabia, the world's largest exporter of crude oil, has partly financed its military spending through increased demand for non-Russian oil and rising oil prices following Russia's invasion of Ukraine. Qatar's military expenditure surged by 27% in 2022, reaching $15.4 billion, marking the steepest growth rate in the Middle East.

Analysis of Investments in Advanced Weapons Systems and Defense Infrastructure

Gulf countries are actively investing in advanced weapons systems and enhancing their defense infrastructure. Saudi Arabia and the UAE, for instance, are establishing their own indigenous defense industries. Saudi Arabia aims to localize 50% of military and security spending by 2030 as part of its Vision 2030 initiative. The UAE has also made significant strides, with its defense exhibition, IDEX, showcasing autonomous systems and artificial intelligence in defense technologies.

These investments are not limited to domestic development. The Gulf states are procuring advanced weapons systems from abroad. Recent acquisitions include the M-SAM air defense system from South Korea by Saudi Arabia and the UAE, and discussions with France for Rafale jets. These procurements reflect a strategic shift to diversify their military suppliers and reduce reliance on traditional partners like the United States.

Examination of Reliance on External Support, Particularly from the United States

The Gulf states have historically relied heavily on the United States for military support and advanced weapons systems. This relationship, however, is evolving due to several factors. Political dynamics, such as the U.S. decision to pull Patriot missiles from Saudi Arabia and freeze the F-35 deal with the UAE, have prompted Gulf countries to seek new partnerships. This shift is evidenced by the increasing presence of non-U.S. firms in the Gulf defense market, with European and Asian companies securing more contracts.

Despite these changes, the U.S. remains a crucial military partner for the Gulf states. The U.S. provides extensive training, maintenance, and support for Gulf military forces. However, the relationship is complicated by U.S. legislative and policy constraints, which sometimes delay or restrict arms sales. For instance, the U.S. Congress has scrutinized arms sales to Saudi Arabia and the UAE due to concerns over human rights and regional stability.

In conclusion, Gulf states are significantly increasing their military expenditures and investing in advanced defense capabilities to enhance their strategic autonomy. While they are diversifying their sources of military technology and reducing reliance on traditional allies like the U.S., the transition is complex and influenced by geopolitical, economic, and strategic factors. The evolving defense landscape in the Gulf highlights a region at a crossroads, seeking to balance traditional alliances with the pursuit of greater self-reliance in defense capabilities.

Sources and References

[1] https://breakingdefense.com/2023/04/saudi-arabia-qatar-see-sharp-jump-in-military-spending-in-the-middle-east-report/

[2] https://www.thenationalnews.com/business/economy/2024/04/21/middle-east-military-burden-is-worlds-highest-in-2023-as-israel-spending-up-24/

[3] https://carnegieendowment.org/sada/79121

[4] https://data.worldbank.org/indicator/MS.MIL.XPND.GD.ZS?locations=1A

[5] https://www.govinfo.gov/content/pkg/CPRT-112SPRT74603/html/CPRT-112SPRT74603.htm

[6] https://www.csis.org/analysis/indigenous-defense-industries-gulf

[7] https://www.heritage.org/military-strength/assessing-the-global-operating-environment/middle-east

[8] https://www.armadainternational.com/2024/02/gulf-defence-industry-shows-its-maturity/

[9] https://www.chathamhouse.org/2020/04/egypt-and-gulf/investment-arms-trade-and-remittances

[10] https://www.csis.org/analysis/gulf-security-looking-beyond-gulf-cooperation-council

[11] https://breakingdefense.com/2023/08/non-us-firms-are-winning-big-deals-in-the-gulf-can-washington-reverse-the-trend/

[12] https://thediplomat.com/2021/06/the-middle-east-an-emerging-market-for-chinese-arms-exports/

[13] https://www.csis.org/analysis/changing-trends-gulf-military-and-security-forces-net-assessment

[14] https://www.globaldata.com/data-insights/aerospace-and-defence/uae-defense-market-budget-assessment-drivers-market-trends-2022/

[15] https://www.marines.mil/Portals/1/Publications/Persian%20Gulf%20States%20Study_1.pdf

[16] https://www.defensenews.com/global/mideast-africa/2018/11/20/whats-standing-in-the-way-of-an-arab-nato/

[17] https://www.washingtoninstitute.org/policy-analysis/israel-normalization-negotiations-and-us-saudi-defense-relationship

[18] https://www.brookings.edu/articles/economic-diversification-in-the-gulf-time-to-redouble-efforts/

[19] https://foreignpolicy.com/2020/10/20/the-uae-is-turning-into-the-world-capital-for-weapons-makers/

[20] https://www2.deloitte.com/xe/en/pages/public-sector/articles/gcc-creation-localized-defense-industry.html

III

Operational Challenges and Ineffectiveness

Institutional weaknesses within Gulf militaries have been a longstanding issue that has hindered their operational effectiveness. These weaknesses stem from various factors, including tribal allegiances within the military hierarchy, lack of meritocratic promotion systems, and corruption. These issues have resulted in a lack of cohesion and unity within Gulf armies, impacting their ability to respond effectively to threats.

Challenges in adapting to unanticipated situations have also plagued Gulf armies. The rigid and hierarchical structure of these military forces often hinders quick decision-making and adaptability to changing circumstances on the battlefield. This inability to be flexible and agile in the face of unexpected challenges has been a significant barrier to their operational success.

Furthermore, deficiencies in critical thinking and personal initiative among ranks have been highlighted as key areas of ineffectiveness within Gulf armies. A culture of top-down command and control has limited the ability of lower-ranking officers and soldiers to exercise independent judgment and take initiative in the field. This lack of empowerment and autonomy has hindered Gulf armies' ability to respond creatively and effectively to complex security threats.

Case studies, such as the Yemeni War, have underscored these operational challenges and inefficiencies within Gulf militaries. The conflict in Yemen has exposed the limitations of Gulf forces in conducting sustained military operations and achieving their strategic objectives. Issues such as logistical shortcomings, coordination problems, and unclear strategic goals have plagued Gulf-led military interventions in the region, highlighting the need for significant reforms and improvements within their armed forces.

Addressing these operational challenges and inefficiencies is crucial for Gulf armies to enhance their military capabilities and effectiveness in the face of evolving security threats in the region. Implementing reforms that promote institutional strength, flexibility, critical thinking, and initiative at all levels of the military hierarchy will be essential for Gulf states to build more agile, adaptive, and responsive armed forces capable of meeting the complex security challenges they face.

In addition to the internal challenges Gulf militaries face, external factors also play a significant role in shaping their operational effectiveness. Gulf states' reliance on foreign suppliers for advanced military technology and equipment has posed a dilemma in terms of operational autonomy and sustainability. While these acquisitions have enhanced the capabilities of Gulf forces regarding firepower and technological sophistication, they have also created dependencies that could undermine their operational effectiveness in the event of supply chain disruptions or geopolitical shifts.

Moreover, the lack of interoperability among Gulf militaries due to differing weapon systems, command structures, and operating procedures has further hindered their ability to collaborate effectively in joint military operations. This lack of standardization and compatibility has limited the effectiveness of multinational military efforts in the region, leading to coordination challenges and inefficiencies during joint exercises and operations.

Additionally, the regional dynamics and security environment in the Gulf have posed unique operational challenges for military forces in the region. The proliferation of non-state actors, transnational threats, and hybrid warfare tactics have necessitated a more nuanced and adaptable approach to security and defense. Gulf armies have struggled to effectively counter these asymmetric threats, often resorting to conventional military strategies that are ill-suited to the complex nature of modern conflicts.

The changing nature of warfare, particularly the shift towards cyber warfare, disinformation campaigns, and unmanned drones, presents additional operational challenges for Gulf militaries. Adversaries increasingly exploit vulnerabilities in cyberspace to disrupt communication networks and manipulate information, requiring Gulf states to enhance their cybersecurity capabilities and develop strategies to mitigate these threats. Additionally, the proliferation of unmanned aerial systems challenges traditional air defense systems, prompting Gulf militaries to invest in advanced anti-drone technologies and tactics.

Furthermore, demographic trends in the Gulf region, such as a growing youth population and high unemployment rates among nationals, present a unique operational challenge for Gulf militaries. Youthful populations may be more susceptible to extremist ideologies and recruitment by terrorist organizations, necessitating comprehensive counter-radicalization efforts and community engagement strategies to prevent the spread of radicalization and violent extremism. Additionally, high levels of youth unemployment can contribute to social unrest and instability, requiring Gulf militaries to address socioeconomic grievances and create opportunities for youth empowerment and inclusion.

In conclusion, addressing the operational challenges and inefficiencies facing Gulf militaries requires a comprehensive and holistic approach that considers internal and external factors shaping their capabilities. Reforms aimed at enhancing institutional strength, promoting flexibility and critical thinking, improving interoperability, adapting to emerging security threats, enhancing cybersecurity capabilities, and addressing socio-economic challenges will be essential for Gulf states to build more resilient and effective armed forces capable of safeguarding regional stability and security.

A. INSTITUTIONAL WEAKNESSES WITHIN GULF MILITARIES

Gulf militaries, despite their significant investments in advanced weaponry and defense capabilities, continue to grapple with institutional weaknesses that hinder their overall efficiency and effectiveness. These weaknesses, deeply ingrained within military structures and operational practices, present formidable challenges to the ability of Gulf armies to fulfill their strategic objectives and protect national security interests.

One of the persistent institutional weaknesses within Gulf militaries is the lack of robust professional military education and training programs. While Gulf states have invested substantially in acquiring sophisticated weapons systems, developing human capital within military ranks has often been neglected. This deficiency in professional education and training can lead to a limited strategic mindset among military leaders, inhibiting their ability to think critically and adapt effectively to complex security threats.

Moreover, the reliance on external defense contractors and foreign advisors to fill critical operational roles within Gulf militaries highlights another institutional weakness: the lack of local expertise and self-reliance. Overreliance on external sources for key functions such as logistics, maintenance, and training can compromise Gulf military forces' autonomy and operational effectiveness, particularly in crises or conflicts where external support may be limited or unavailable.

Additionally, challenges related to interoperability and coordination among Gulf military forces pose significant institutional hurdles to effective joint operations and coalition-building efforts. The lack of standardized protocols, communication systems, and joint training exercises can impede the seamless integration of diverse military assets and hinder the synergistic use of resources in multi-dimensional military campaigns.

Furthermore, patronage networks, nepotism, and favoritism within Gulf military establishments can undermine merit-based promotions, erode morale among rank-and-file personnel, and breed internal dissent and factionalism. These detrimental practices not only compromise the cohesion and unity of military units but also jeopardize the overall combat readiness and operational capabilities of Gulf armies.

To address these institutional weaknesses effectively, Gulf states must prioritize comprehensive reforms that focus on enhancing professional military education, developing local expertise, cultivating a culture of self-reliance, promoting interoperability among military branches, and fostering a meritocratic and transparent system of leadership and governance. By investing in human capital development, institutional capacity-building, and strategic thinking, Gulf militaries can overcome their inherent weaknesses and position themselves as capable and agile regional security and stability defenders.

B. CHALLENGES IN ADAPTING TO UNANTICIPATED SITUATIONS

In addressing unanticipated situations, the Gulf region presents a unique set of challenges for military forces due to its complex security environment characterized by geopolitical rivalries, historical animosities, and ongoing conflicts. The strategic location of the Gulf states along key maritime chokepoints and energy transit routes makes them vulnerable to a variety of threats, including interstate tensions, terrorism, proxy warfare, and cyber attacks. This volatile landscape necessitates high readiness and flexibility for Gulf armies to respond to sudden and unpredictable security crises effectively.

One of the key obstacles facing Gulf military forces in adapting to unforeseen circumstances is the legacy of traditional warfare paradigms that prioritize conventional capabilities over asymmetric and hybrid threats. Historically, Gulf states have focused on building their armed forces with advanced weapon systems, large standing armies, and external security partnerships to deter conventional threats from regional adversaries. However, the evolving nature of modern warfare, marked by non-state actors, irregular warfare tactics, and information warfare, requires a shift towards more flexible and agile defense capabilities that can effectively counter various challenges.

Moreover, the lack of a comprehensive and integrated approach to defense planning and resource allocation within Gulf military establishments hampers their ability to anticipate and respond to emerging security threats proactively. Oftentimes, bureaucratic inertia, siloed decision-making processes, and stovepiped information flows inhibit the timely exchange of intelligence and coordination between different branches of the armed forces, leading to fragmented responses and suboptimal outcomes in crises. This organizational rigidity can undermine the agility and adaptability of Gulf armies in dealing with rapidly evolving security dynamics that demand swift and coordinated actions on multiple fronts.

Furthermore, the reliance of Gulf states on foreign military assistance, including arms sales, training programs, and deployment of foreign troops, raises questions about the extent of their self-reliance and sovereign capabilities in managing unexpected security challenges. While external partnerships can provide valuable resources and expertise to bolster Gulf defense capabilities, they also introduce dependencies and vulnerabilities that may limit the autonomy and flexibility of Gulf armies in responding to crises without foreign support. Striking a balance between leveraging external partnerships and building local capabilities is essential for Gulf states to enhance their resilience and responsiveness in the face of unanticipated security threats.

In light of these complex dynamics, Gulf militaries are increasingly recognizing the need to adapt their defense strategies, organizational structures, and operational doctrines to meet the multifaceted challenges of the contemporary security landscape. Embracing a more holistic and forward-thinking approach to defense planning and preparedness, Gulf armies can enhance their ability to anticipate, prevent, and mitigate the impacts of unforeseen security crises, thereby safeguarding the stability and prosperity of the region in an era of heightened uncertainty and volatility.

C. DEFICIENCIES IN CRITICAL THINKING AND PERSONAL INITIATIVE AMONG RANKS

One key factor contributing to deficiencies in critical thinking and personal initiative among Gulf armies is the historical context in which these military forces have evolved. Gulf states have often faced threats from external adversaries and internal dissent, leading to a strong emphasis on regional security and stability. This has resulted in military structures that prioritize hierarchy, discipline, and centralized command and control to ensure a unified response to potential threats.

While this approach may have advantages in maintaining order and cohesion, it can also inadvertently suppress individual initiative and creativity among military personnel. The emphasis on obedience and adherence to orders can create a culture where questioning authority or proposing alternative courses of action is discouraged, limiting the ability of frontline troops to think critically and adapt to changing circumstances.

Moreover, the rapid modernization and expansion of Gulf militaries in recent years have placed additional pressure on personnel to acquire new skills and capabilities quickly. This focus on technical proficiency and operational efficiency can sometimes come at the expense of developing broader problem-solving, decision-making, and strategic thinking competencies.

Another aspect that exacerbates the challenges of critical thinking and personal initiative within Gulf armies is the prevalence of bureaucratic hurdles and cumbersome decision-making processes. A complex web of regulations, protocols, and approval mechanisms can slow down the flow of information and impede timely responses to emerging threats or opportunities on the battlefield.

To address these issues, Gulf armies must cultivate a culture that values and rewards critical thinking, innovation, and independent action among all ranks. This can be achieved through targeted training programs focusing on developing cognitive skills, fostering creativity, and encouraging continuous improvement. Additionally, creating mechanisms for feedback, open communication, and active participation in decision-making processes can empower personnel to contribute their unique perspectives and expertise to mission planning and execution.

By promoting a culture of adaptability, flexibility, and individual empowerment within Gulf armies, these military forces can enhance their operational effectiveness and readiness to meet the complex security challenges of the region. Embracing a more holistic approach to talent development and leadership, Gulf states can better position their armed forces to navigate the uncertainties of the modern security landscape and effectively protect their national interests.

Furthermore, incorporating design thinking principles and agile methodologies into military planning and operations can help Gulf armies foster a mindset of continuous adaptation and innovation. These approaches emphasize the importance of experimentation, rapid prototyping, and learning from failure, enabling military personnel to respond more effectively to dynamic and unpredictable threats in today's fast-paced security environment.

Additionally, investing in the professional development of military officers and NCOs to enhance their decision-making skills, strategic insight, and intercultural competence can further strengthen Gulf armies' capacity to think critically and act decisively in complex operational scenarios. By nurturing a cadre of forward-thinking leaders empowered to challenge conventional wisdom and explore new approaches to problem-solving, Gulf states can build more agile and resilient military forces capable of meeting the evolving security challenges of the 21st century.

D. CASE STUDIES ILLUSTRATING OPERATIONAL CHALLENGES, SUCH AS THE YEMENI WAR

In this expanded section, we will further analyze the operational challenges faced by Gulf armies in the Yemeni War, looking into the complexities and nuances that shape their military interventions.

One of the central operational challenges confronting Gulf armies in the Yemeni War is the arduous task of achieving their military objectives in the face of a resilient and adaptive opponent. The Houthi rebels, deeply entrenched in Yemen, have demonstrated a remarkable ability to effectively employ guerrilla tactics and asymmetrical warfare strategies to thwart Gulf-led offensives. This has placed significant strain on the conventional capabilities of Gulf armies, raising fundamental questions about the appropriateness and efficacy of their military strategies in the Yemeni context.

Logistical constraints represent a formidable obstacle for Gulf armies operating in Yemen. The vast and rugged terrain, challenging weather conditions, and limited infrastructure present profound difficulties in sustaining and supporting military operations over prolonged periods. Disrupted supply chains, inadequate transportation routes, and the need to maneuver personnel, equipment, and vital supplies through hostile environments all contribute to the immense logistical challenges that Gulf forces confront in Yemen. These logistical hurdles hamper the operational tempo of military activities and impact the overall sustainability and effectiveness of Gulf military operations in Yemen.

Furthermore, coordination issues among the diverse elements of the Gulf armed forces complicate operational effectiveness in the Yemeni theater. The integration and synchronization of air, land, and sea forces from multiple Gulf states necessitate seamless communication, close cooperation, and efficient coordination to advance unified military objectives. However, differences in operational doctrines, equipment interoperability challenges, and command structure variations can impede the cohesive coordination required for successful joint military operations. The need for improved interoperability and synergy among different components of Gulf armies remains a critical priority in addressing operational challenges in Yemen.

The involvement of external actors, most notably Iran, introduces an additional layer of complexity to the operational environment in Yemen. Iran's alleged support for the Houthi rebels, characterized by the provision of weapons, training, and financial aid, has escalated tensions in the region and fostered a proxy warfare dynamic that further complicates the conflict landscape. The presence of external actors with vested interests introduces intricate geopolitical considerations and strategic challenges that Gulf armies must navigate while conducting military operations in Yemen.

In sum, the operational challenges confronting Gulf armies in the

Yemeni War underscore the imperative for a comprehensive and adaptive approach to military interventions. By addressing the complexities associated with achieving military objectives, overcoming logistical constraints, enhancing coordination among diverse elements of the armed forces, and effectively managing external influences, Gulf armies can enhance their operational effectiveness and fortify their capabilities to confront and resolve complex conflicts in the future.

IN A NUTSHELL

> **Institutional Weaknesses within Gulf Militaries**
>
> Gulf militaries have historically faced institutional weaknesses that have impeded their operational effectiveness. These weaknesses are multifaceted and deeply rooted in the political and social structures of the Gulf states. One of the primary issues is the influence of tribal allegiances within the military hierarchy, which often supersedes merit and capability in promoting and assigning military personnel. This tribalism undermines the meritocracy essential for a competent and professional military force. The lack of a meritocratic promotion system means that individuals are often promoted based on their tribal affiliations or royal connections rather than their skills or performance. This can lead to the appointment of less competent individuals to key positions, which affects the overall operational capability of the military.
>
> Corruption is another significant challenge within Gulf militaries. Resources are sometimes misallocated for personal gain rather than being used to enhance military capabilities. This corruption can also manifest in the procurement process,

where contracts may be awarded based on personal connections rather than the quality or suitability of the equipment or services being procured.

Challenges in Adapting to Unanticipated Situations

Gulf militaries often struggle to adapt to unanticipated situations due to rigid command structures and a lack of flexibility in decision-making. The hierarchical nature of these militaries, where orders are expected to be followed without question, can stifle individual initiative and critical thinking. This can be particularly problematic in rapidly evolving combat situations where lower-ranking officers and soldiers may be reluctant to take the initiative or make decisions without explicit orders from above.

Deficiencies in Critical Thinking and Personal Initiative Among Ranks

Gulf militaries' educational and training systems have been criticized for not fostering critical thinking and personal initiative. The emphasis on rote learning and memorization rather than analytical skills and problem-solving means that military personnel may be ill-equipped to deal with complex or unexpected challenges. Cultural factors that discourage questioning authority or deviating from established procedures can exacerbate this deficiency.

Case Studies Illustrating Operational Challenges, Such as the Yemeni War

The ongoing conflict in Yemen provides a stark illustration of the operational challenges faced by Gulf militaries, particularly the Saudi-led coalition. Despite significant investments in advanced weaponry and military technology, the coalition has faced difficulties in achieving its strategic objectives. The war has highlighted issues such as inadequate ground force capabilities, over-reliance on air power, and challenges in coordinating operations among coalition partners. The humanitarian impact of the conflict, including civilian casualties and widespread destruction, has also raised questions about the effectiveness of the coalition's military strategy and its adherence to international humanitarian law.

In conclusion, Gulf militaries face various institutional and operational challenges that hinder their effectiveness. Tribalism, lack of meritocracy, corruption, and deficiencies in training and education all contribute to these challenges. The war in Yemen serves as a case study that underscores the consequences of these issues, demonstrating the need for comprehensive reform within Gulf military institutions to enhance their operational capabilities and effectiveness.

Sources and References

[1] https://democracyparadox.com/2021/11/22/why-the-armies-of-arabia-remain-weak-institutions/

[2] https://www.csis.org/analysis/changing-trends-gulf-military-and-security-forces-net-assessment

[3] https://carnegieendowment.org/files/war_in_saada.pdf

[4] https://www.cfr.org/backgrounder/yemen-crisis

[5] https://agsiw.org/five-climate-challenges-the-gulf-states-might-not-have-time-to-solve/

[6] https://aoav.org.uk/2023/case-studies-saudi-arabia-in-yemen-assessing-the-effectiveness-of-the-arms-trade-treaty-part-8/

[7] https://sohs.alnap.org/system/files/content/resource/files/main/SOHS%202018%20Yemen%20CS.pdf

[8] https://www.chathamhouse.org/2020/07/risk-perception-and-appetite-uae-foreign-and-national-security-policy-0/8-case-study-uae

[9] https://www.csis.org/analysis/military-officers-gulf-career-trajectories-and-determinants

[10] https://academic.oup.com/book/39793/chapter-abstract/339893654?redirectedFrom=fulltext

[11] https://gulfif.org/gcc-states-security-as-the-councils-turns-into-a-failed-institution/

[12] https://www.ennonline.net/attachments/2459/Yemen-Case-Study.pdf

[13] https://www.meforum.org/441/why-arabs-lose-wars

[14] https://www.chathamhouse.org/sites/default/files/publications/research/2019-05-30-Gulf%20Crisis_0.pdf

[15] https://economic-research.bnpparibas.com/html/en-US/Gulf-countries-challenge-energy-transition-3/9/2023,48341

[16] https://unctad.org/news/red-sea-crisis-and-implications-trade-facilitation-africa

[17] https://www.elibrary.imf.org/view/journals/002/2023/413/article-A001-en.xml

[18] https://www.ncbi.nlm.nih.gov/pmc/articles/PMC6878400/

[19] https://www.samhsa.gov/sites/default/files/military_white_paper_final.pdf

[20] https://www.elibrary.imf.org/view/journals/007/2022/052/article-A001-en.xml

IV

Comparative Military Strength

In the context of the Middle East's complex geopolitical landscape, the comparative military strength of Gulf states plays a crucial role in shaping regional security dynamics. Various indices and methodologies rank military powers, providing valuable insights into each country's defense capabilities and preparedness. Factors such as defense spending, personnel numbers, equipment holdings, and operational capabilities are key considerations in these rankings.

Gulf states, including Saudi Arabia, the United Arab Emirates, and Qatar, consistently feature prominently in regional military power assessments. These countries have invested significantly in modernizing their armed forces, acquiring advanced weaponry, and enhancing their combat capabilities through training and joint exercises. Saudi Arabia, for instance, boasts one of the largest defense budgets in the world and has made substantial investments in acquiring cutting-edge military technologies.

Gulf states often face unique challenges and considerations compared to other major regional powers like Iran, Israel, and Turkey. Iran's large population, asymmetric warfare capabilities, and regional influence present a notable counterbalance to Gulf state military strength. Israel's sophisticated defense industry, technological advancements, and strategic partnerships further complicate the regional military balance. Meanwhile, Turkey's growing military assertiveness, strategic positioning, and ambitions for regional leadership add another layer of complexity to the equation.

The implications of these rankings for military effectiveness are manifold. Understanding where Gulf states stand about their neighbors enables policymakers and military planners to identify strategic priorities, prioritize resource allocation, and tailor defense strategies accordingly. It also helps anticipate potential security threats, assess interoperability with coalition partners, and enhance deterrence capabilities in a volatile and unpredictable region.

As Gulf states navigate a range of security challenges, including regional conflicts, terrorism, maritime security threats, and ballistic missile proliferation, their military strength remains a critical factor in safeguarding national interests and preserving regional stability. By continually evaluating and enhancing their military capabilities, Gulf states can better position themselves to address emerging threats, project power regionally, and contribute to collective security efforts in the Middle East.

The evolving nature of warfare and security threats in the region underscores the importance of adaptive military strategies and agile defense postures for Gulf states. Non-traditional security challenges, such as cyber warfare, terrorism, and proxy conflicts, require innovative and comprehensive responses beyond traditional military capabilities. Gulf states are increasingly investing in capabilities related to these emerging threats, including establishing cyber defense units, enhancing counterterrorism capabilities, and participating in multinational security initiatives to address common challenges collaboratively.

Furthermore, the regional dynamics in the Gulf are constantly shaped by external influences, including great power competition, arms sales, and security partnerships. Global powers like the United States, Russia, and China in the region add another layer of complexity to the security environment, influencing defense strategies and military planning for Gulf states. Balancing relations with multiple external actors while safeguarding national sovereignty and security interests presents a delicate diplomatic and strategic challenge for Gulf leaders.

In sum, Gulf states' military strength remains critical to regional security dynamics in the Middle East. By continually investing in modernization, training, and strategic partnerships, Gulf states can enhance their defense capabilities, project regional stability, and contribute to collective security efforts. Adaptability, innovation, and collaboration are key pillars for Gulf states to navigate the evolving security landscape and address emerging threats effectively in the pursuit of peace and stability in the Middle East.

A. INTRODUCTION TO INDICES RANKING MILITARY POWERS IN THE MIDDLE EAST

Background on Gulf states' military investments

The Gulf states have a long history of investing heavily in their military capabilities. This trend can be traced back to the colonial era when these countries sought to modernize their armed forces to protect their territories and resources. Today, the Gulf states continue to place a strong emphasis on defense spending, with many of them having some of the highest military budgets in the world. These investments have been driven by a variety of factors, including regional security threats, geopolitical rivalries, and the desire to assert themselves on the world stage.

Importance of assessing Gulf armies' efficiency

Given the significant resources that Gulf states allocate to their military, it is crucial to assess the efficiency and effectiveness of their armed forces. This is important not only for the countries themselves to ensure that they are getting the best return on their investments but also for regional and international security considerations. A well-trained and well-equipped military can deter potential adversaries, protect vital interests, and contribute to regional stability.

Overview of key dimensions examined in the book

We will delve into several key dimensions to assess the efficiency of Gulf states' armies. This includes examining their organizational structure, command and control mechanisms, training and readiness levels, technological capabilities, and overall strategic posture.

Regarding organizational structure, Gulf armies often have a hierarchical system that emphasizes centralized command and control. This structure is designed to facilitate rapid decision-making and coordination of efforts during times of crisis. However, it also sometimes leads to bureaucratic inefficiencies and delays in response, especially when faced with non-traditional security threats such as asymmetric warfare or cyber-attacks.

In terms of training and readiness levels, Gulf states have made significant investments in building professional and well-trained military forces. Many of them send their personnel to foreign training programs and participate in joint exercises with allies to enhance their skills and capabilities. Nevertheless, there may still be gaps in training programs that do not adequately address emerging threats or incorporate the latest tactics and technologies.

Technological capabilities are also a key aspect of assessing military efficiency. Gulf states have been keen on acquiring advanced weapons systems and technologies from various international suppliers to modernize their arsenals. While this has bolstered their combat capabilities, there are concerns about interoperability between different systems and the sustainability of maintaining such high-tech assets over the long term.

Finally, the strategic posture of Gulf armies is influenced by a complex web of regional rivalries, alliances, and security challenges. Some states prioritize defense cooperation with Western powers, while others seek to bolster their defenses through strategic partnerships with other regional actors. Balancing these competing interests and determining the most effective defense posture requires carefully considering both internal and external security dynamics.

B. ANALYSIS OF GULF STATES' RANKINGS VIS-À-VIS REGIONAL POWERS

1. Overview of Gulf states' military spending trends

The Gulf states, comprising countries such as Saudi Arabia, the

United Arab Emirates (UAE), Qatar, Kuwait, Bahrain, and Oman, have long been known for their significant investments in bolstering their military capabilities. The region's geopolitical dynamics, including regional rivalries, security threats, and concerns over Iran's influence, have been key drivers of the Gulf states' defense spending trends.

Over the past few decades, Gulf states have consistently allocated substantial portions of their budgets to defense expenditures. Saudi Arabia, in particular, has one of the highest defense budgets in the world, reflecting its status as a key player in regional security arrangements. The UAE has also emerged as a major military spender, seeking to diversify its defense capabilities and reduce its reliance on traditional security partners.

2. Analysis of investments in advanced weapons systems and defense infrastructure

The Gulf states' investments in advanced weapons systems and defense infrastructure have been aimed at enhancing their military capabilities and deterring potential threats. Advanced fighter jets, missile defense systems, armored vehicles, naval vessels, and surveillance technology are among the key acquisitions made by Gulf countries to modernize their armed forces.

Saudi Arabia has notably procured advanced weapons systems such as F-15 fighter jets, Patriot missile defense systems, and Eurofighter Typhoon aircraft, signaling its commitment to maintaining a robust defense posture. The UAE has also invested heavily in cutting-edge military technology, including sophisticated drones, missile systems, and combat aircraft, to ensure its regional military superiority.

Furthermore, Gulf states have focused on developing domestic defense industries and infrastructure to reduce their dependence on foreign suppliers. Countries like the UAE and Saudi Arabia have established defense manufacturing facilities and research centers, fostering local capabilities in areas such as cyber security, aerospace, and defense technology innovation.

3. Examination of reliance on external support, particularly from the United States

While the Gulf states have made significant strides in enhancing their military capabilities through investments in advanced weaponry and domestic defense industries, they continue to rely heavily on external support, primarily from the United States. The US has been a key security partner for Gulf countries, providing arms sales, military training, and strategic cooperation to bolster the region's defense capabilities.

The presence of US military bases in countries such as Bahrain, Qatar, and the UAE further underscores the deep security ties between the Gulf states and the United States. Arms sales agreements, such as the multi-billion-dollar deals between the US and Saudi Arabia, have enabled Gulf countries to acquire high-tech military hardware and maintain interoperability with US forces.

However, while external support has been instrumental in strengthening the Gulf states' defense capabilities, it also raises concerns about their armed forces' long-term sustainability and strategic autonomy. Recent shifts in US foreign policy priorities and calls for greater burden-sharing by regional partners have prompted Gulf countries to reassess their defense strategies and explore more diversified security partnerships.

In conclusion, the Gulf states' military spending trends, investments in advanced weapons systems, and reliance on external support underscore the complex dynamics shaping the region's security landscape. By balancing internal modernization efforts with strategic partnerships, Gulf countries aim to safeguard their interests, deter potential threats, and maintain stability in a volatile security environment.

C. IMPLICATIONS OF RANKINGS FOR MILITARY EFFECTIVENESS

In assessing the rankings of Gulf states' military power in the Middle East, it is essential to delve deeper into the intricate web of factors that shape their military capabilities. While quantitative indicators like defense spending, troop numbers, and weapon inventories certainly provide a valuable snapshot of military strength, a more nuanced analysis must consider qualitative elements underpinning operational effectiveness and combat readiness.

One critical aspect to consider is the doctrinal coherence and strategic thinking level within Gulf states' armed forces. A clear and well-articulated military doctrine, aligned with national security objectives and informed by realistic threat assessments, can guide force structuring, training priorities, and procurement decisions. Furthermore, the ability of military leaders to adapt and innovate in response to evolving security challenges is paramount in ensuring operational agility and effectiveness.

The role of human capital in shaping military power cannot be overstated. Recruitment, training, and retention of skilled personnel across all ranks are essential for maintaining a high-performance military force. Investing in professional military education, leadership development programs, and talent management systems can cultivate a cadre of competent and motivated service members capable of executing complex missions and adapting to dynamic operational environments.

Moreover, military readiness encompasses more than just hardware and personnel. Critical enablers such as logistics, sustainment capabilities, and infrastructure must be robust and resilient to support military operations effectively. Maintaining a solid industrial base, fostering innovation in defense technologies, and establishing partnerships with domestic and international suppliers are key to building a sustainable military capability.

The importance of strategic partnerships and alliances in enhancing Gulf states' military power cannot be overlooked. Collaborating with like-minded nations in joint exercises, information sharing, and capacity-building initiatives can strengthen interoperability and foster regional security cooperation. Moreover, leveraging these partnerships to access advanced military technologies, intelligence support, and training opportunities can enhance Gulf armies' overall effectiveness and deterrence posture.

In conclusion, a holistic understanding of the complex factors that shape Gulf states' military power is essential for accurately assessing their rankings in the Middle East. By focusing on doctrinal clarity, human capital development, readiness infrastructure, and strategic partnerships, Gulf states can fortify their military capabilities and position themselves to address the region's multifaceted security challenges. Embracing a forward-looking approach to military modernization and readiness will safeguard Gulf states' strategic interests and national security in an increasingly complex and uncertain strategic landscape.

IN A NUTSHELL

Introduction to Indices Ranking Military Powers in the Middle East

Military power indices provide a systematic approach to evaluating and comparing countries' military capabilities. These indices, such as the Global Firepower Index (GFP), use a combination of over 60 factors to calculate a nation's Power Index ('PwrIndx') score. The factors considered include military personnel numbers, equipment holdings, financial conditions, logistical capabilities, and geographic positions. These indices are crucial for understanding the relative military strength of nations within the Middle East, offering insights into their defense readiness and strategic positioning.

Analysis of Gulf States' Rankings Vis-à-Vis Regional Powers

In the context of the Middle East, Gulf states show varied rankings in terms of military power. According to the 2024 GFP rankings, countries like Saudi Arabia and the UAE are among the top military powers in the region. For instance, Saudi Arabia has a Power Index score of 0.3235, making it one of the more vital military forces in the Gulf, mainly due to its substantial defense budget and significant investments in modern military technology. The UAE follows closely with a score of 0.8083, reflecting its well-funded defense sector and advanced military assets.

Other regional powers, such as Turkey and Iran, also feature prominently in these rankings. Turkey leads with a Power Index score of 0.1697, attributed to its extensive military personnel and advanced military technology. Iran follows with a score of 0.2269, supported by its large armed forces and indigenous military industry. These rankings illustrate the strategic military balance in the region, highlighting the Gulf states' positions relative to their larger neighbors.

Implications of Rankings for Military Effectiveness

The rankings have significant implications for the military effectiveness of Gulf states. Firstly, the high rankings of countries like Saudi Arabia and the UAE indicate a solid conventional military capability, which is crucial for deterrence and regional influence. However, the effectiveness of these military forces is not solely determined by their rankings. Operational effectiveness also depends on factors such as command structure, personnel training, and the ability to conduct joint operations, areas where Gulf states have faced challenges.

Moreover, the rankings influence geopolitical dynamics in the Middle East. High military rankings can enhance a country's bargaining power in international and regional politics, affecting alliances and diplomatic engagements. For Gulf states, this means an ability to assert more influence in regional conflicts and negotiations, such as the ongoing tensions with Iran and involvement in conflicts like the Yemeni war.

In conclusion, military power indices provide a valuable framework for assessing the comparative military strengths of Gulf states within the broader Middle East region. These rankings highlight the substantial military capabilities and strategic positions of Gulf states like Saudi Arabia and the UAE. However, the actual military effectiveness of these states also depends on qualitative factors beyond mere numerical rankings, influencing their role and efficacy in regional security dynamics.

Sources and References

[1] https://en.tempo.co/read/1827951/10-middle-east-countries-with-strongest-militaries-in-2024
[2] https://www.newarab.com/news/turkey-egypt-and-iran-top-mena-military-firepower-rankings
[3] https://www.globalfirepower.com/countries-listing-persian-gulf-powers.php
[4] https://www.globalfirepower.com/countries-listing-middle-east.php
[5] https://www.arabnews.com/node/2443461/middle-east
[6] https://www.al-monitor.com/originals/2023/01/middle-east-military-rankings-turkey-highest-lebanon-lowest-global-index
[7] https://uklandpower.com/2018/11/07/do-we-need-to-simplify-the-rank-structures-of-uk-armed-forces/
[8] https://www.forbes.com/sites/dominicdudley/2018/02/26/ten-strongest-military-forces-middle-east/?sh=6f6754c316a2
[9] https://scholarworks.waldenu.edu/cgi/viewcontent.cgi?article=11601&context=dissertations
[10] https://www.ncbi.nlm.nih.gov/pmc/articles/PMC7274300/
[11] https://digitalcommons.odu.edu/cgi/viewcontent.cgi?article=1005&context=gpis_etds
[12] https://www.businessinsider.in/politics/slidelist/44951441.cms
[13] https://www.globalfirepower.com/countries-listing.php
[14] https://en.wikipedia.org/wiki/Arab_states_of_the_Persian_Gulf
[15] https://gmi.bicc.de
[16] https://onlinelibrary.wiley.com/doi/10.1111/mepo.12731?af=R

[17] https://www.tandfonline.com/doi/full/10.1080/19480881.2023.2261206
[18] https://www.jstor.org/stable/45294364
[19] https://www.tandfonline.com/doi/abs/10.1080/21635781.2020.1717689
[20] https://www.jstor.org/stable/2539118

V

Internal and External Security Challenges

Gulf states in the Middle East region face a myriad of internal security threats that not only challenge their stability and sovereignty but also shape their geopolitical landscape. These threats emanate from a complex interplay of factors, ranging from terrorism and extremist ideologies to governance uncertainties and socio-political disparities.

The presence of extremist groups, such as ISIS and Al-Qaeda, has posed a significant challenge to the internal security of Gulf states. These groups have exploited political and social grievances and sectarian tensions to further their radical agendas and undermine government authority. The threat of terrorism has necessitated a multi-faceted approach to counter-radicalization, border security, intelligence-sharing, and law enforcement coordination within Gulf states.

Moreover, internal security challenges are intertwined with governance uncertainties and divisions prevalent in the Gulf region.

Authoritarian regimes, tribal allegiances, and dynastic rule have created power dynamics that can fuel internal rivalries and exacerbate social tensions. The lack of political pluralism and limited avenues for civic engagement have also contributed to disenchantment among population segments, leading to sporadic outbreaks of unrest and dissent.

In addition to internal threats, Gulf states face a complex web of external security challenges that shape their strategic calculus. The rivalry with Iran, rooted in historical animosities, ideological differences, and competing regional ambitions, has been a dominant factor driving Gulf states' security policies. Iran's support for proxy groups and its pursuit of regional hegemony have heightened security concerns and created a volatile environment characterized by proxy conflicts and covert operations.

Furthermore, regional conflicts, such as the protracted civil war in Yemen and the devastating conflict in Syria, have had a profound impact on the security landscape of Gulf states. Gulf countries' involvement in these conflicts, through military interventions and support for various factions, has not only escalated tensions but also exposed them to direct security threats, including cross-border attacks and retaliatory measures. The humanitarian toll of these conflicts has exacerbated socio-economic challenges and created fertile ground for radicalization and recruitment by extremist groups.

Addressing the complex array of internal and external security threats facing Gulf states requires a holistic approach that encompasses security sector reform, governance reforms, regional cooperation, and diplomatic initiatives to de-escalate tensions and foster stability. Enhancing resilience, fostering social cohesion, and promoting inclusive governance structures are essential in building a secure and prosperous future for Gulf states amidst their challenges.

The interconnectedness of these security challenges underscores the importance of comprehensive strategies that address the root causes of instability, promote inclusive development, and strengthen cooperation among Gulf states and regional partners. By addressing the intertwined issues of terrorism, governance deficiencies, and external threats in a coordinated and collaborative manner, Gulf states can enhance their resilience and chart a more stable and secure future for their citizens and the broader region.

A. OVERVIEW OF INTERNAL SECURITY THREATS FACED BY GULF STATES

Gulf states in the Middle East deal with numerous internal security threats. These threats demand careful planning and strategic action to stabilise the region and protect national security. The reasons behind these threats are complicated and involve political, social, economic, and ideological factors. This mix creates a tough situation for those in charge of governance and security.

One of the key internal security threats confronting Gulf states is the potential for political unrest and social upheaval. Grievances against ruling regimes, economic disparities, lack of political freedoms, and aspirations for greater democratic participation often fuel this threat. The Arab Spring uprisings that swept across the region in 2011 served as a stark reminder of the vulnerability of Gulf states to popular dissent and demands for political reform.

Terrorism remains a persistent threat to internal security in the Gulf region, with extremist groups such as ISIS and Al-Qaeda exploiting societal grievances and sectarian tensions to sow chaos and advance their radical agendas. Gulf states have been targeted by terrorist attacks in the past, leading to heightened security measures and increased cooperation with international partners to counter the threat of violent extremism.

Ethnic and sectarian divisions also pose a significant challenge to internal security in certain Gulf states, especially those with diverse populations, such as Bahrain and Saudi Arabia. Tensions between Sunni and Shia Muslims, as well as other minority groups, can inflame social unrest and threaten the fragile balance of social cohesion and political stability in these countries. Efforts to address these divisions through inclusive policies and inter-communal dialogue are essential for mitigating the risk of sectarian violence.

In addition to these internal challenges, Gulf states grapple with security risks posed by transnational organized crime, cyber-attacks, and foreign interference in their domestic affairs. The illicit trafficking of weapons, drugs, and humans, as well as cyber threats targeting critical infrastructure and sensitive information, further complicate efforts to combat internal security threats and maintain law and order.

Addressing these multifaceted internal security challenges requires a comprehensive and integrated approach encompassing effective governance, inclusive policies, robust law enforcement capabilities, and community engagement. Gulf states must prioritize efforts to address underlying grievances, promote social cohesion, enhance intelligence sharing and counterterrorism cooperation, and strengthen their security infrastructure to effectively counter internal security threats and preserve their sovereignty in the face of evolving risks.

In recent years, the emergence of new security challenges, including the impact of the COVID-19 pandemic, climate change, and cyber warfare, has added further complexity to the internal security landscape in the Gulf region. The pandemic has strained healthcare systems and exacerbated social and economic inequalities, leaving populations vulnerable to exploitation by extremist groups and criminal networks. Additionally, the effects of climate change, such as water scarcity and food insecurity, can fuel social tensions and exacerbate existing vulnerabilities, posing a threat to the overall stability of Gulf states.

Moreover, the increasing sophistication and frequency of cyber attacks targeting government institutions, critical infrastructure, and private businesses have raised concerns about the potential for disruptive and destructive cyber operations that could undermine national security and economic stability. Gulf states invest in cybersecurity measures and capabilities to enhance their resilience against these emerging threats and protect their digital infrastructure from malicious actors seeking to exploit vulnerabilities for political or financial gain.

As Gulf states navigate these multifaceted internal security challenges and adapt to new and evolving threats, policymakers and security agencies must adopt a proactive and holistic approach to safeguarding their nations' stability, prosperity, and sovereignty. By addressing the root causes of internal security threats, promoting social cohesion, fostering international cooperation, and investing in advanced security capabilities, Gulf states can strengthen their resilience and effectively mitigate the risks posed by complex security dynamics in the region.

B. GOVERNANCE UNCERTAINTIES AND DIVISIONS

Gulf states have faced longstanding challenges related to governance uncertainties and divisions, which can significantly impact the efficiency and effectiveness of their military forces. These issues are deeply rooted in the region's political, social, and historical contexts.

One key aspect contributing to governance uncertainties in Gulf states is the concentration of power in ruling families or elites. This concentration of power can lead to internal rivalries, power struggles, and factionalism within the military and broader governance structures. The lack of precise mechanisms for succession and decision-making can further exacerbate these uncertainties, as uncertainty about leadership transitions can create instability and weaken the overall coherence of the military.

Furthermore, the complex tribal dynamics present in many Gulf societies can also influence governance and military affairs. Tribal allegiances and rivalries often cut across formal military structures, leading to challenges in fostering a cohesive and unified military force. Tribal networks can sometimes precede official hierarchies, undermining discipline and effectiveness within the armed forces. Additionally, historical grievances or disputes among tribes can spill over into military operations, complicating decision-making processes and reducing operational efficiency.

In addition to internal factors, external influences play a significant role in shaping governance uncertainties and divisions within Gulf states. Regional power dynamics, such as competition between Saudi Arabia and Iran, can impact Gulf states' governance structures and military strategies. The involvement of external actors, whether through arms sales, military support, or intervention in domestic affairs, can further complicate governance dynamics and contribute to divisions within the military.

Addressing governance uncertainties and divisions requires a multifaceted approach that tackles deep-seated issues of power dynamics, tribal relations, and external influences. Reforms aimed at promoting transparency, accountability, and inclusivity in governance structures are crucial for strengthening the resilience and effectiveness of Gulf militaries. Building a sense of national identity and unity among diverse populations is essential for fostering cohesion within the armed forces and enhancing their readiness to respond to security challenges.

Addressing governance uncertainties and divisions within Gulf states is a complex and ongoing process that requires strategic leadership, institutional reforms, and a commitment to building a strong and unified military force. By addressing these challenges head-on, Gulf states can enhance their defense capabilities and safeguard their national security in an increasingly volatile region.

C. EXTERNAL SECURITY CHALLENGES, INCLUDING TENSIONS WITH IRAN

The external security landscape in the Gulf region is intricately linked with the historical and ongoing tensions between the Gulf states and Iran. This chapter delves deeper into the complex dynamics of this relationship, exploring the root causes, key events, and evolving strategies that shape the security environment in the region.

Historical Context:

The tensions between Gulf states and Iran have historical roots that date back centuries. The Persian Gulf has been a contested strategic region due to its geographic significance and rich energy resources. Competition for control and influence has been a constant feature, with various empires, kingdoms, and modern states vying for regional dominance. The historical animosities between Persians and Arabs, as well as the Sunni-Shia divide, have exacerbated tensions and shaped the geopolitical landscape of the Gulf.

Key Events and Flashpoints:

The Iranian Revolution of 1979 was a seismic event that reshaped the balance of power in the region. The overthrow of the Shah and the establishment of the Islamic Republic of Iran introduced a revolutionary regime that challenged the existing order and sought to export its ideology beyond its borders. The revolution marked a turning point in Iran's relations with its Arab neighbors, sparking fears of destabilization and revolution in the Gulf monarchies. The Iran-Iraq War from 1980 to 1988 further strained relations, as Gulf states supported Iraq against Iran, fearing the spread of the Islamic Revolution.

Subsequent flashpoints, such as the 1983 bombing of the U.S. Marine barracks in Beirut by Hezbollah, an Iranian-backed militant group, and the 1987-1988 "Tanker War" in the Persian Gulf, highlighted the volatility and unpredictability of the security environment in the region. The Gulf states' concerns over Iran's support for militant proxies and its nuclear program have deepened mistrust and fueled a cycle of threats and countermeasures.

Military Postures and Defense Strategies:

In response to Iran's perceived threats, Gulf states have embarked on ambitious military modernization programs to enhance their defense capabilities. Saudi Arabia and the United Arab Emirates, in particular, have acquired advanced weaponry, including fighter jets, missile defense systems, and surveillance technology, to counter potential threats from Iran. The formation of the Gulf Cooperation Council (GCC) in 1981 was a pivotal step towards collective security cooperation among Gulf states, aimed at countering external threats and promoting regional stability.

Through establishing military bases and defence agreements, the presence of U.S. military forces in the region has been a cornerstone of Gulf states' defense strategies. The U.S. has played a crucial role in providing security assurances, training, and intelligence support to Gulf allies, while also pursuing its own strategic interests in the region, including safeguarding energy flows and countering Iranian influence.

Impact on Regional Stability:

The tensions between Gulf states and Iran have had profound implications for regional stability and security. The ongoing conflicts in Syria, Iraq, and Yemen have become arenas of competition between Gulf states and Iran, fueling proxy wars and exacerbating humanitarian crises. The 2015 Iran nuclear deal, known as the Joint Comprehensive Plan of Action (JCPOA), aimed at curbing Iran's nuclear program in exchange for sanctions relief, generated both hopes for diplomatic rapprochement and fears of increased Iranian assertiveness in the region.

The strategic competition between Iran and Gulf states has heightened the risks of conflict escalation and military confrontation, with potential implications for global energy markets and maritime security in the Gulf. The sabotage of oil tankers, drone attacks on key infrastructure, and missile strikes on Gulf cities underscore the volatility and vulnerability of the region to asymmetric threats and disruptive tactics. The proliferation of ballistic missiles and drone technology among non-state actors further complicates the security landscape, posing challenges for defense planners and policymakers.

Diplomatic Engagements and Conflict Resolution Efforts:

Amidst the security challenges posed by tensions with Iran, Gulf states have sought to engage in diplomatic initiatives and conflict resolution efforts to de-escalate tensions and promote regional stability. Diplomatic channels, such as the Gulf Dialogue and the Arab League, have facilitated dialogue, confidence-building measures, and crisis management between Gulf states and Iran. Multilateral forums, including the United Nations and the Organization of Islamic Cooperation, have also addressed common security concerns and promoted peaceful coexistence in the region.

Addressing the root causes of regional tensions, such as sectarian divisions, political grievances, and socio-economic disparities, is crucial for building sustainable peace and security in the Gulf. Confidence-building measures, crisis communication mechanisms, and track-two dialogues can help create conflict prevention and resolution channels. Regional initiatives like the Riyadh Summit and the Manama Dialogue provide platforms for dialogue and cooperation among Gulf states, Iran, and other stakeholders to address shared security challenges and promote regional stability.

In sum, the tensions between Gulf states and Iran continue to shape the external security landscape in the region, with historical animosities, military rivalries, and geopolitical ambitions driving complex dynamics. By understanding the historical context, key events, military strategies, and diplomatic efforts, we gain insights into the challenges and opportunities for enhancing regional security and fostering cooperation among Gulf states, Iran, and external partners. Sustaining dialogue, building trust, and investing in conflict prevention mechanisms are essential steps towards mitigating risks and advancing the cause of peace in the Gulf region.

D. IMPACT OF REGIONAL CONFLICTS ON GULF STATES' SECURITY LANDSCAPE

Regional conflicts have been a longstanding feature of the geopolitically complex Gulf region, with many factors interplaying to shape the security landscape of the Gulf states. The prevalence of conflicts in neighboring countries, such as the ongoing civil war in Syria, the protracted conflict in Yemen, and the security challenges in Iraq, has underscored the vulnerability of Gulf states to external threats and instability. These regional conflicts have posed direct security risks and exacerbated existing fault lines and amplified sectarian tensions in the region.

The security implications of regional conflicts are manifested in various ways, including the proliferation of non-state actors, the spread of extremist ideologies, and the disruption of social cohesion within Gulf societies. The influx of refugees and internally displaced persons from conflict-affected countries has strained resources, infrastructure, and social services in Gulf states, leading to social and economic challenges. Furthermore, the transnational nature of security threats from regional conflicts requires a coordinated regional approach to counter-terrorism, counter-extremism, and border security.

The geopolitical competition in the Middle East, particularly between Gulf states and Iran, adds another layer of complexity to the security landscape. The rivalry between Saudi Arabia and Iran, supported by their respective allies and proxies, has fueled regional polarization and proxy conflicts, further heightening tensions and insecurity in the Gulf region. The strategic maneuvers and power plays of external actors, including the United States, Russia, and European powers, have also contributed to the intricate web of alliances and rivalries that shape regional security dynamics.

Economically, the Gulf states are not immune to the ripple effects of regional conflicts, particularly regarding energy security and economic stability. The disruption of energy supplies, the volatility of oil prices, and the potential for economic sanctions due to regional tensions all challenge Gulf states' economic prosperity and financial well-being. Diversifying economies and investment portfolios and promoting regional economic cooperation are essential strategies for mitigating the economic risks posed by regional conflicts.

Ultimately, Gulf states' security landscapes are deeply intertwined with the dynamics of regional conflicts, requiring a nuanced and multidimensional approach to addressing the complex challenges posed by external threats, geopolitical rivalries, and economic vulnerabilities. By fostering regional dialogue, cooperation, and conflict resolution mechanisms, Gulf states can strive to enhance their security resilience and promote stability in the volatile Middle East region.

The historical context of regional conflicts in the Gulf can be traced back to colonial legacies, post-colonial nation-building processes, and the interplay of tribal, sectarian, and ideological fault lines. The geopolitical significance of the Gulf region, characterized by its vast energy reserves, strategic location, and maritime chokepoints, has attracted the attention of global powers seeking to exert influence and secure their interests. The legacy of Cold War rivalries, the Arab-Israeli conflict, and the Iranian Revolution of 1979 have all left lasting imprints on the security dynamics of the Gulf states.

The ongoing conflicts in Syria, Yemen, and Iraq have had far-reaching implications for the security environment of the Gulf region, fueling proxy wars, arms races, and humanitarian crises. The Syrian civil war, in particular, has drawn in regional and international actors, leading to a complex web of alliances and interventions that have further destabilized the region. The conflict in Yemen, characterized by a Saudi-led military intervention against Houthi rebels, has underscored the strategic competition between Saudi Arabia and Iran, exacerbating sectarian tensions and humanitarian suffering.

The spread of extremist ideologies, terrorism, and radicalization stemming from regional conflicts poses a direct threat to the security and stability of Gulf states. The rise of groups such as ISIS and Al-Qaeda in the region has necessitated enhanced cooperation in intelligence sharing, counter-terrorism measures, and border security to prevent the spillover of violence and extremism into Gulf territories. The social and economic impact of conflicts, including displacement, unemployment, and loss of livelihoods, has created vulnerable populations susceptible to recruitment by extremist groups.

The role of external actors in shaping the security landscape of the Gulf cannot be underestimated, with major powers such as the United States, Russia, China, and European states pursuing their strategic interests in the region. The US military presence in the Gulf, through bases in countries such as Bahrain, Qatar, and Kuwait, has been a source of contention and cooperation with Gulf states in addressing security threats. Meanwhile, Russia's involvement in conflicts such as Syria and its arms sales to Gulf countries have added a new dimension to the regional power dynamics.

In response to the complex security challenges posed by regional conflicts, Gulf states have pursued a mix of diplomatic, military, and humanitarian initiatives to mitigate risks and promote stability. The Gulf Cooperation Council (GCC), established in 1981, serves as a platform for regional dialogue, crisis management, and security cooperation among member states. Military alliances, such as the Saudi-led coalition in Yemen and the US-led maritime security coalition in the Gulf, aim to address shared security threats and enhance deterrence capabilities.

The economic dimensions of regional conflicts, including the impact on oil markets, investment flows, and trade routes, have significant implications for the economic resilience of Gulf states. The diversification of economies away from oil dependence, investment in infrastructure and technology, and promotion of regional economic integration are critical strategies for safeguarding against economic shocks resulting from regional conflicts. Moreover, efforts to address the root causes of conflicts, such as political grievances, sectarian tensions, and economic disparities, are essential for sustainable peace and security in the Gulf region.

In sum, the security landscape of Gulf states is shaped by a complex interplay of historical, geopolitical, and economic factors that influence regional conflicts and their ramifications. By addressing the root causes of insecurity, strengthening regional cooperation, and fostering a comprehensive approach to conflict resolution, Gulf states can enhance their security resilience and contribute to stability in the volatile Middle East region.

IN A NUTSHELL

Overview of Internal Security Threats Faced by Gulf States

Gulf states face a range of internal security threats that significantly impact their stability and governance. These threats include terrorism, extremist ideologies, and internal dissent, which are often exacerbated by socioeconomic disparities and rapid modernization efforts. The presence of extremist groups influenced by radical ideologies poses a significant threat, as these groups often seek to exploit political grievances and social inequalities. Additionally, the rapid pace of social change and the challenges of integrating diverse populations contribute to internal security concerns, as they can lead to social unrest and challenge traditional governance structures.

Governance Uncertainties and Divisions

Governance in the Gulf states is marked by uncertainties and divisions that stem from the traditional tribal and familial structures of political power. These uncertainties are often highlighted by the lack of transparency and accountability in governance, which can lead to corruption and nepotism. Moreover, the Gulf states' reliance on oil revenues has led to economic disparities exacerbating governance challenges, as economic downturns can quickly translate into political grievances. The political systems in many Gulf states are also characterized by a lack of public participation in the political process, which can lead to feelings of disenfranchisement and increase the risk of internal unrest.

External Security Challenges, Including Tensions with Iran

Externally, Gulf states are continually navigating a complex regional security environment dominated by their rivalry with Iran. This rivalry extends beyond mere political disagreements, encompassing religious, territorial, and strategic dimensions. Iran's influence in the region, through its support for proxy groups in countries like Yemen, Iraq, and Lebanon, poses a direct challenge to the security and influence of Gulf states. The nuclear ambitions of Iran further complicate this relationship, adding a layer of nuclear security concerns that Gulf states must address within their regional security strategies.

Impact of Regional Conflicts on Gulf States' Security Landscape

Regional conflicts, notably the ongoing conflict in Yemen and the broader tensions between Iran and other major powers have a profound impact on the security landscape of the Gulf states. The war in Yemen, in particular, has become a significant security concern for Saudi Arabia and the UAE, as it is seen as a direct threat to their southern borders and has led to missile and drone attacks on their territories. These conflicts strain military resources and pose humanitarian and reputational risks. Furthermore, the involvement of Gulf states in these conflicts often leads to international criticism and can complicate their relationships with global powers.

In conclusion, Gulf states face a multifaceted security environment characterized by internal and external challenges. Internal threats stem from socio-political disparities and governance issues, while external threats are largely defined by the strategic rivalry with Iran and the impact of regional conflicts. These challenges require comprehensive security strategies that address both the symptoms and root causes of instability, ensuring both national and regional security.

Sources and References

[1] https://carnegieendowment.org/2021/05/18/reassuring-gulf-partners-while-recalibrating-u.s.-security-policy-pub-84522
[2] https://apps.dtic.mil/sti/tr/pdf/ADA346280.pdf
[3] https://apps.dtic.mil/sti/tr/pdf/ADA555928.pdf
[4] https://www.wilsoncenter.org/event/changing-landscape-gulf-cooperation-council-security
[5] https://www.csis.org/analysis/changing-trends-gulf-military-and-security-forces-net-assessment
[6] https://www.brookings.edu/articles/securing-the-persian-gulf-washington-must-manage-both-external-aggression-and-internal-instability/
[7] https://mepc.org/journal/internal-and-external-security-arab-gulf-states
[8] https://warontherocks.com/2023/10/gulf-states-should-push-iran-to-get-serious-about-lowering-tensions/
[9] https://www.csis.org/analysis/security-challenges-and-threats-gulf-0
[10] https://www.scirp.org/journal/paperinformation?paperid=130572
[11] https://www.atlanticcouncil.org/region/the-gulf/
[12] https://democracyjournal.org/magazine/36/understanding-the-gulf-states/
[13] https://www.theguardian.com/world/2024/apr/19/gulf-states-response-to-iran-israel-conflict-may-decide-outcome-of-crisis
[14] https://www.cfr.org/global-conflict-tracker/conflict/confrontation-between-united-states-and-iran
[15] https://www.washingtoninstitute.org/policy-analysis/gulf-navigates-multipolar-world

[16] https://www.ncbi.nlm.nih.gov/pmc/articles/PMC8483429/
[17] https://www.wilsoncenter.org/article/contemporary-security-challenges-and-peace-landscape-gulf-and-mena-region
[18] https://www.bloomberg.com/news/articles/2024-04-17/saudis-and-uae-warn-of-war-dangers-as-israel-iran-tensions-boil
[19] https://www.imf.org/en/Blogs/Articles/2023/12/01/middle-east-conflict-risks-reshaping-the-regions-economies
[20] https://www.elibrary.imf.org/view/journals/002/2023/413/article-A001-en.xml

VI

Evaluating Training and Personnel

Efficient training programs play a crucial role in developing the skills and capabilities of military personnel within Gulf armies. Training equips soldiers with the necessary knowledge and expertise to perform their duties effectively and ensures readiness for a range of operational scenarios. By investing in comprehensive training programs, Gulf states can enhance their armed forces' overall efficiency and effectiveness.

Training programs within Gulf armies are designed to cover various essential skills, including weapons proficiency, tactical maneuvers, communication techniques, and situational awareness. These programs often incorporate realistic training exercises, simulations, and live-fire drills to simulate combat conditions and prepare soldiers for the challenges they may face.

Furthermore, modern training methodologies such as virtual reality simulations, computer-based learning modules, and distance education programs have been integrated into training regimens to enhance the effectiveness of instruction and provide soldiers with opportunities to practice and refine their skills in a controlled environment.

In addition to technical skills, training programs also focus on fostering leadership abilities, teamwork, decision-making under pressure, and adaptability in rapidly changing circumstances. These soft skills are essential for military personnel to respond to dynamic and unpredictable situations effectively and work cohesively to achieve mission objectives.

Regular training and professional development are essential to maintaining a high level of readiness and operational effectiveness within Gulf armies. By continually investing in the training and development of their personnel, Gulf states can ensure that their armed forces remain prepared, capable, and responsive to the region's evolving security challenges.

Moreover, training plays a vital role in enhancing the professionalization of Gulf military forces, instilling a culture of discipline, dedication, and commitment among service members. Through structured training programs, soldiers learn the technical skills required for their roles and the values and ethics essential for upholding the integrity and honor of the armed forces.

The evolution of training techniques in recent years has also emphasised adaptive learning approaches, personalized training plans, and continuous assessment to tailor instruction to individual needs and maximize learning outcomes. By leveraging advancements in technology and educational methodologies, Gulf armies can provide their personnel with cutting-edge training experiences that are immersive, engaging, and effective in preparing them for the complex and dynamic nature of modern warfare.

In sum, the significance of training in enhancing military efficiency cannot be overstated. By prioritizing robust and innovative training programs, Gulf states can ensure that their armed forces are well-prepared, highly skilled, and agile in responding to the ever-changing security landscape. Investing in the development and professionalization of military personnel through training not only strengthens the capabilities of Gulf armies but also reinforces their ability to fulfill their defense responsibilities effectively and safeguard the region's security.

A. THE ROLE OF TRAINING IN ENHANCING MILITARY EFFICIENCY

Training is crucial in enhancing military efficiency and effectiveness within Gulf armies. A well-trained and skilled military force is better equipped to respond to various operational challenges, adapt to dynamic environments, and achieve mission success. Training's role extends beyond the individual level to encompass unit cohesion, leadership development, and overall organizational capabilities.

The effectiveness of military training programs is contingent upon several key factors. Firstly, the curriculum must be tailored to address Gulf armies' specific needs and challenges, considering regional security dynamics, technological advancements, and evolving warfare tactics. Training should cover various skills, including combat training, equipment operation, strategic planning, and coordination with allied forces.

Furthermore, the quality of training instructors and mentors is paramount in shaping the capabilities of military personnel. Experienced trainers with a deep understanding of military operations can impart valuable knowledge, skills, and best practices to trainees, helping them to excel in their roles. Mentorship programs that pair experienced personnel with newer recruits can also promote knowledge transfer and professional development, fostering a culture of continuous learning within the military organization.

Additionally, using cutting-edge training technologies, simulation tools, and virtual reality platforms can enhance the realism and effectiveness of training exercises. Virtual simulations allow soldiers to practice tactical maneuvers, engage in virtual combat scenarios, and familiarize themselves with complex equipment in a safe and controlled environment. By simulating real-world situations, soldiers can develop critical thinking, problem-solving, and decision-making skills essential for success in the field.

Regular and ongoing training is essential to maintaining readiness and proficiency among military personnel. Continuous training allows soldiers to hone their skills, adapt to new challenges, and stay abreast of emerging threats. Beyond technical skills, training also plays a crucial role in fostering mental resilience, emotional intelligence, and ethical decision-making among soldiers, promoting a holistic approach to military readiness.

In recent years, Gulf armies have increasingly prioritized joint training exercises and interoperability with allied forces to enhance operational effectiveness and regional security cooperation. These joint exercises strengthen military capabilities and foster relationships and trust among participating nations, paving the way for more effective joint responses to shared security challenges.

Furthermore, adopting modern training methodologies, such as blended learning approaches and adaptive training technologies, can optimize the learning experience for military personnel. Blended learning models combine traditional classroom instruction with online resources, interactive modules, and self-paced tutorials, allowing soldiers to learn quickly and reinforce key concepts through different mediums.

Ultimately, the role of training in enhancing military efficiency cannot be overstated. Investments in high-quality training programs, experienced instructors, mentorship initiatives, and advanced technologies are critical to building a capable and resilient military force in the Gulf region. By prioritizing training and professional development, Gulf armies can enhance their operational effectiveness, readiness, and overall effectiveness in addressing security challenges and safeguarding national interests.

B. ASSESSING THE QUALITY OF PERSONNEL WITHIN GULF ARMIES

Assessing the quality of personnel within Gulf armies is a multifaceted and essential aspect of evaluating these military forces' operational effectiveness and combat readiness. The Gulf states have long recognized the significance of having well-trained, skilled, and motivated personnel to meet the evolving security challenges in the region. The quality of personnel within Gulf armies is influenced by several key factors, including recruitment practices, training programs, leadership development, and retention strategies.

Recruitment practices in Gulf armies vary across the region, with some countries implementing mandatory conscription while others rely on voluntary enlistment. Conscription can ensure a steady inflow of manpower into the military but may not always result in a highly skilled or motivated force. On the other hand, voluntary enlistment allows for a more selective recruitment process, enabling Gulf states to attract individuals with specialized skills and expertise that are crucial for modern warfare. Additionally, Gulf states have started to explore alternative recruitment methods, such as tapping into the growing pool of female candidates to diversify their forces and benefit from a wider range of talents and perspectives.

Training programs are pivotal in shaping the quality of military personnel within Gulf armies. These programs encompass various skills and knowledge areas, including combat tactics, marksmanship, physical fitness, military ethics, and communication. Gulf states often collaborate with international military training institutions to access cutting-edge training methodologies and best practices, ensuring that their personnel receive world-class instruction and are well-prepared for the complexities of modern warfare. Furthermore, technological advancements have enabled Gulf states to incorporate virtual reality simulations and other innovative training tools to enhance the effectiveness of their training programs and provide realistic scenarios for personnel to hone their skills.

Leadership development is another critical factor in assessing personnel quality within Gulf armies. Effective leadership is essential for maintaining morale, discipline, and operational efficiency among military units. Gulf states invest in leadership training to develop a cadre of competent officers capable of making sound decisions under pressure, inspiring their troops, and effectively leading them in combat situations. Strong leadership enhances unit cohesion, fosters a culture of professionalism, and contributes to overall mission success. In recent years, Gulf states have prioritized developing leadership skills relevant to the evolving nature of modern warfare, such as adaptability, strategic thinking, and the ability to leverage technological advancements to gain a tactical advantage.

Retention strategies play a crucial role in retaining high-quality personnel within Gulf armies. Offering competitive salaries, benefits, and career advancement opportunities can help increase morale and job satisfaction among military personnel. Moreover, creating a positive work environment that emphasizes camaraderie, teamwork, and a sense of purpose can enhance retention rates and foster a deep commitment to serving the nation. Gulf states have implemented innovative retention strategies, such as providing educational opportunities, healthcare benefits, and support for military families, to incentivize personnel to stay in the military and contribute to its long-term success. By prioritizing these retention efforts, Gulf states can build a stable and highly skilled workforce dedicated to safeguarding national security and promoting regional stability.

C. STRATEGIES FOR IMPROVING TRAINING PROGRAMS AND PERSONNEL CAPABILITIES

In addition to the strategies outlined in the preceding section, there are several other key considerations that Gulf armies should consider to further enhance their training programs and personnel capabilities. Leveraging data analytics and cyber technologies can revolutionize military training by providing valuable insights into performance, resource allocation, and operational effectiveness. By collecting and analyzing data on training outcomes, Gulf armies can gain a deeper understanding of their strengths and weaknesses, enabling them to tailor training programs to specific needs and maximize resource utilisation efficiency.

Implementing advanced cyber technologies in training simulations can significantly enhance the realism and complexity of exercises, ensuring that military personnel are well-prepared to counter emerging cyber threats in an ever-evolving digital landscape. Immersive and interactive training scenarios replicating real-world challenges can enhance critical thinking, decision-making skills, and operational readiness, equipping Gulf armies with the capabilities to respond effectively to cyber warfare and information operations.

Furthermore, prioritizing mental health and resilience initiatives is essential for building a workforce equipped to cope with the demands and stresses of military service. Providing comprehensive mental health resources, promoting psychological well-being, and fostering a culture of support can enhance morale, productivity, and overall readiness among military personnel. Training in stress management techniques, resilience-building strategies, and emotional regulation can empower individuals to effectively navigate high-pressure situations, reducing the risk of burnout and improving their capacity to perform under challenging circumstances.

Promoting diversity and inclusion within military ranks is imperative for cultivating a cohesive and inclusive organizational culture that values all personnel's diverse backgrounds, perspectives, and experiences. Embracing diversity can foster a culture of creativity, innovation, and collaboration, enabling Gulf armies to leverage the full spectrum of talent and skills within their ranks. By creating an environment where all individuals feel respected, valued, and included, Gulf armies can enhance team cohesion, boost morale, and ultimately enhance operational effectiveness in diverse and complex operational environments.

Moreover, integrating cross-cultural training and language proficiency programs can enhance the readiness and effectiveness of Gulf military personnel in multinational operations and engagements with foreign partners. Proficiency in foreign languages and cross-cultural awareness can facilitate effective communication, collaboration, and coordination with allied forces and international partners, enhancing interoperability and mission success in diverse operational contexts. By investing in cross-cultural competency and language skills, Gulf armies can strengthen their ability to operate effectively in multinational coalitions and achieve shared objectives in complex, dynamic security environments.

In conclusion, by incorporating these additional considerations into their training programs and personnel development strategies, Gulf armies can elevate their operational capabilities, enhance their readiness, and fortify their resilience in the face of evolving security challenges. Embracing data analytics, cyber technologies, mental health and resilience initiatives, diversity and inclusion efforts, and cross-cultural training programs can enable Gulf states to build a highly adaptable and effective military force capable of navigating the complexities of modern warfare and achieving success in diverse operational environments.

IN A NUTSHELL

The Role of Training in Enhancing Military Efficiency

Training plays a critical role in enhancing the efficiency of military forces by ensuring that personnel are well-prepared to execute their duties effectively and respond to various challenges. Regular and rigorous training programs help maintain a high state of readiness and operational capability, which is essential for the effectiveness of military operations. Training encompasses a wide range of activities, from basic combat skills to advanced technological and leadership training, all aimed at improving the tactical and strategic capabilities of the armed forces.

Assessing the Quality of Personnel within Gulf Armies

The quality of personnel in Gulf armies is a pivotal factor in determining their overall effectiveness and efficiency. This quality is assessed based on several criteria, including the level of education, the rigor of training, and the ability to perform complex tasks under pressure. Studies indicate that well-educated and rigorously trained troops are significantly more effective on the battlefield. For Gulf states, enhancing the educational standards and training rigor for military personnel is crucial. This involves basic military training and specialized training in areas such as intelligence, logistics, and cyber warfare, which are increasingly important in modern military operations.

Strategies for Improving Training Programs and Personnel Capabilities

To improve training programs and enhance the capabilities of personnel within Gulf armies, several strategies can be employed:

1. **Integration of Advanced Technologies**: Incorporating advanced technologies such as simulators, virtual reality (VR), and digital training tools can provide soldiers with realistic and diverse training scenarios. These technologies help develop critical thinking and decision-making skills under simulated combat conditions.

2. **Joint and Multinational Training Exercises**: Participating in joint and multinational training exercises can expose Gulf military personnel to various operational tactics and procedures. These exercises enhance interoperability and tactical proficiency by learning from other armies' experiences and best practices.

3. **Continuous Professional Development**: Establishing continuous professional development programs that include leadership training, technical skills enhancement, and strategic thinking workshops can significantly improve the quality of military personnel. These programs should be tailored to

the needs of the military and aligned with the strategic objectives of the Gulf states.

4. **Feedback and Adaptation**: Training programs should be regularly assessed and adapted based on performance feedback and changing security dynamics. This adaptive approach ensures that the training remains relevant and effective in preparing military personnel for current and future challenges.

5. **Educational Partnerships**: Gulf states can benefit from partnerships with military academies and educational institutions worldwide to enhance their training programs. These partnerships can facilitate the exchange of knowledge, expertise, and resources, thereby elevating the standard of training and education available to Gulf military personnel.

In conclusion, the effectiveness of Gulf armies heavily relies on the quality of their training programs and the capabilities of their personnel. By investing in advanced training technologies, participating in joint exercises, promoting continuous professional development, and leveraging international partnerships, Gulf states can significantly enhance their armed forces' operational readiness and efficiency. Given its complex geopolitical landscape, these measures are essential for maintaining security and stability in the region.

Sources and References

[1] https://www.airuniversity.af.edu/Portals/10/ASPJ/journals/Volume-26_Issue-1/Feature-Weiss.pdf

[2] https://www.rand.org/content/dam/rand/pubs/research_reports/RRA1600/RRA1658-1/RAND_RRA1658-1.pdf

[3] https://core.ac.uk/download/pdf/12118101.pdf

[4] https://www.cfc.forces.gc.ca/259/290/308/192/ali.pdf

[5] https://www.tandfonline.com/doi/full/10.1080/10242694.2020.1851474

[6] https://digitalcommons.pepperdine.edu/cgi/viewcontent.cgi?article=1222&context=etd

[7] https://iea.org.uk/publications/the-case-for-markets-in-defence-driving-efficiency-and-effectiveness-in-military-spending/

[8] https://www.ncbi.nlm.nih.gov/pmc/articles/PMC8427986/

[9] https://rfpb.defense.gov/Portals/67/Documents/Reports/RFPB%20Improving%20the%20Total%20Force%202020%20Report_1.pdf?ver=LB1TBW7DQnIf-_pP_9scag%3D%3D

[10] https://assets.publishing.service.gov.uk/media/5a815450e5274a2e8ab5364d/The_Report_of_the_Iraq_Inquiry_-_Volume_XII.pdf

[11] https://sustainabledevelopment.un.org/content/documents/20161UAE_SDGs_Report_Full_English.pdf

[12] https://tdhj.org/blog/post/data-driven-decision-making-military/

[13] https://apps.dtic.mil/sti/pdfs/ADA249270.pdf

[14] https://www.orsam.org.tr/d_hbanaliz/Kitap_Serisi-1-2.pdf

[15] https://www.dla.mil/Portals/104/Documents/Headquarters/History/EffectivenessAndEfficiency1Sept2021.pdf

[16] https://www.ncbi.nlm.nih.gov/pmc/articles/PMC5238493/
[17] https://www.nato.int/cps/en/natohq/topics_111830.htm
[18] https://www.imf.org/external/pubs/ft/sdn/2014/sdn1412.pdf
[19] https://www.researchgate.net/publication/216155927_The_Efficiency_Aspect_of_Military_Effectiveness

VII

Utilization of Technology and Innovation

The Gulf states have made significant strides in modernizing their military capabilities by harnessing cutting-edge technology and integrating it into their operations. This continuous pursuit of technological advancement has transformed the Gulf armies and positioned them as key players in the global defense arena. Through deploying state-of-the-art weapons systems, advanced surveillance technology, and innovative communication networks, Gulf states have redefined how military operations are conducted in the region.

One critical area where the integration of cutting-edge technology has had a profound impact is enhancing situational awareness. Gulf nations have invested heavily in advanced reconnaissance and surveillance assets, including unmanned aerial vehicles (UAVs), satellites, and high-tech sensors, to gather real-time intelligence on potential threats and monitor adversaries. Accessing timely and accurate information has empowered Gulf commanders to make strategic decisions swiftly and effectively respond to emerging security challenges.

Moreover, cutting-edge technology has significantly improved the precision and efficacy of Gulf military engagements. The acquisition of precision-guided munitions, advanced targeting systems, and missile defense capabilities has revolutionized how Gulf forces engage hostile targets, enabling them to deliver precise strikes with minimal collateral damage. This precision enhances the operational success of military missions and underscores the Gulf states' commitment to minimizing civilian casualties and upholding humanitarian principles in conflict zones.

In addition to enhancing offensive capabilities, the integration of advanced technology has bolstered Gulf states' defensive posture against evolving threats. Developing robust cyber warfare capabilities, sophisticated electronic warfare systems, and secure communication networks has fortified Gulf defenses against cyberattacks, electronic warfare, and information warfare. By investing in cutting-edge cybersecurity measures and training personnel in modern warfare techniques, Gulf nations have elevated their readiness and resilience in the face of emerging security challenges.

While the progress in integrating cutting-edge technology into Gulf military operations is commendable, ongoing challenges must be addressed to realize the full potential of these advancements. Gulf states are working to develop local research and development capabilities, reduce reliance on foreign suppliers for critical technologies, and enhance training programs to build a skilled workforce capable of operating and maintaining advanced military equipment. Collaboration with international partners, investment in local innovation hubs, and the continuous pursuit of technological advancements will be pivotal in overcoming these challenges and sustaining the momentum of modernization in Gulf militaries.

Ultimately, the integration of cutting-edge technology has propelled Gulf armies to new operational capabilities and fortified their position as strategic players in the global defense landscape. By leveraging advanced technologies, enhancing situational awareness, and strengthening defensive capabilities, Gulf states can navigate complex security challenges and maintain their standing as dynamic and influential military forces in the region and beyond.

A. INTEGRATION OF CUTTING-EDGE TECHNOLOGY IN GULF MILITARY OPERATIONS

Technology Integration in Gulf Military Operations:

The utilization of cutting-edge technology has become a cornerstone of Gulf military operations, reshaping the strategic landscape and augmenting the capabilities of regional armed forces. Gulf states have embarked on a significant modernization drive, investing heavily in advanced technological solutions to enhance their combat readiness, operational effectiveness, and deterrence posture. This extended chapter delves deeper into the multifaceted aspects of technology integration in Gulf military operations, exploring key developments, challenges, and strategic implications.

Advanced Weapons Systems and Platforms:

Gulf states have invested substantially in acquiring and deploying advanced weapons systems and platforms to bolster their military capabilities. From next-generation fighter jets and precision-guided missiles to advanced naval vessels and air defense systems, the region has witnessed a proliferation of cutting-edge weaponry. The integration of these advanced systems has augmented the firepower of Gulf militaries and increased their operational reach and strategic depth.

Moreover, developing and deploying local defense technologies have emerged as a key priority for Gulf states, fostering technological self-reliance and enhancing national defense capabilities. Collaborative ventures with international defense contractors and establishing domestic defense industries have enabled Gulf countries to customize advanced weapon systems to meet their unique operational requirements.

Information Fusion and Command, Control, Communications, Computers, Intelligence, Surveillance, and Reconnaissance (C4ISR):

Integrating information fusion and advanced C4ISR capabilities has fundamentally transformed how Gulf militaries conduct operations. Armed forces in the region have achieved unprecedented situational awareness and operational agility by leveraging real-time data analytics, satellite imagery, signals intelligence, and networked communication systems. The seamless integration of disparate sensors, platforms, and communication networks has enabled commanders to make informed decisions rapidly, coordinate joint operations efficiently, and respond effectively to dynamic threats.

Furthermore, the convergence of artificial intelligence, machine learning, and big data analytics has revolutionized the processing and exploitation of vast amounts of information, enabling Gulf militaries to extract actionable intelligence and gain a decisive edge in information superiority. The development of integrated C4ISR networks, secure communication systems, and advanced data encryption protocols have reinforced the resilience of Gulf military operations against cyber threats and electronic warfare challenges.

Future Trends and Strategic Outlook:

The trajectory of technology integration in Gulf military operations is poised to continue evolving rapidly, driven by advancements in emerging technologies such as quantum computing, unmanned systems, hypersonic weapons, and autonomous platforms. The convergence of these disruptive technologies is expected to reshape warfare in the region, posing both opportunities and challenges for Gulf states.

In unmanned systems, the proliferation of swarming drones, autonomous ground vehicles, and unmanned maritime vessels is anticipated to revolutionize surveillance, reconnaissance, and strike capabilities, opening up new possibilities for decentralized and distributed operations. Integrating artificial intelligence and machine learning algorithms into autonomous systems will enhance decision-making processes, optimize resource allocation, and enable adaptive responses to dynamic battlefield conditions.

Moreover, the growing emphasis on network-centric warfare, multi-domain operations, and joint force integration is expected to shape the future of military strategy and operations in the Gulf region. Integrating air, land, sea, space, and cyber capabilities into a seamless and interconnected operational framework will enable Gulf militaries to project power, deter adversaries, and counter emerging threats effectively.

In conclusion, the relentless pursuit of technological innovation and integration in Gulf military operations underscores the region's commitment to maintaining strategic superiority, enhancing deterrence capabilities, and safeguarding national interests in an increasingly complex security environment. As Gulf states navigate the complexities of modern warfare and embrace the transformative potential of advanced technologies, the convergence of innovative solutions, institutional reforms, and strategic investments will be critical in shaping the region's future trajectory of military modernization and operational excellence.

B. INNOVATIONS IMPACTING THE EFFICIENCY OF GULF ARMIES

Innovations in military technology have played a pivotal role in transforming the capabilities and readiness of Gulf armies, shaping their strategic posture and enhancing their operational effectiveness across diverse security scenarios. The relentless pursuit of cutting-edge defense capabilities and the integration of advanced technologies have positioned Gulf states as formidable military forces in the region, capable of responding decisively to complex security challenges and emerging threats.

One key area of innovation that has significantly bolstered the military prowess of Gulf armies is the adoption of advanced weapons systems. Gulf states have invested heavily in acquiring state-of-the-art fighter jets, missile defense systems, and precision-guided munitions to strengthen their firepower and deter potential adversaries. The deployment of advanced aircraft such as the F-15 Eagle, F-16 Fighting Falcon, and Eurofighter Typhoon has enhanced the air superiority capabilities of Gulf air forces, allowing them to conduct aerial combat missions with unprecedented precision and agility.

Moreover, integrating sophisticated missile defense systems, including Patriot batteries and THAAD, has bolstered the strategic defense capabilities of Gulf states, providing them with a robust shield against ballistic missile threats and enhancing their ability to protect critical infrastructure and population centers. The continuous modernization of weapon systems and the adoption of cutting-edge technologies have ensured that Gulf armies remain at the forefront of military innovation, capable of projecting power and deterring regional aggression.

In addition to advanced weapons systems, Gulf armies have also leveraged surveillance and reconnaissance technologies to enhance their intelligence-gathering capabilities and situational awareness on the battlefield. The deployment of surveillance drones, satellites, and advanced sensors has provided military commanders with real-time information, enabling them to monitor enemy movements, track hostile activities, and execute precision strikes with unmatched precision and efficiency. These advanced surveillance assets have revolutionized the way Gulf armies conduct reconnaissance missions, gather intelligence, and respond to emerging threats in dynamic operational environments.

Furthermore, integrating modern communication and command systems has played a crucial role in improving the coordination, collaboration, and decision-making processes within Gulf armies. Implementing advanced C4ISR technologies has enabled seamless connectivity, real-time information sharing, and centralized command structures, enhancing the overall effectiveness and responsiveness of Gulf military forces. By leveraging cutting-edge communication systems, Gulf armies are better equipped to coordinate complex operations, facilitate rapid decision-making, and ensure seamless interoperability among different branches of the military.

Moreover, the growing emphasis on cyber warfare capabilities has positioned Gulf states at the forefront of cybersecurity innovation, enabling them to defend against cyber threats, protect critical infrastructure, and conduct offensive cyber operations against potential adversaries. The development of robust cyber defense measures, including advanced encryption protocols, network security systems, and threat intelligence platforms, has bolstered the resilience of Gulf armies against cyber attacks and information warfare, safeguarding their command and control systems, communication networks, and sensitive data from unauthorized access and manipulation.

Additionally, Gulf armies have embraced the transformative potential of training and simulation technologies to enhance military personnel's skills, readiness, and performance in diverse operational scenarios. Adopting virtual reality simulations, advanced training facilities, and cutting-edge simulation tools has enabled soldiers to practice complex tactical maneuvers, hone their decision-making skills, and improve their teamwork and cohesion in simulated combat environments. By integrating state-of-the-art training methodologies, Gulf armies strive to ensure that their forces are well-prepared, adaptable, and capable of responding effectively to evolving security challenges and dynamic battlefield conditions.

Furthermore, the integration of autonomous and unmanned systems has revolutionized the way Gulf armies conduct military operations, enabling them to leverage the capabilities of unmanned aerial vehicles (UAVs), unmanned ground vehicles (UGVs), and autonomous maritime vessels for a wide range of missions, including reconnaissance, surveillance, strike operations, and logistics support. These unmanned systems provide Gulf states with enhanced situational awareness, operational flexibility, and precision engagement capabilities, allowing them to conduct missions with reduced risk to human life, extend their operational reach, and maintain persistent surveillance over critical areas of interest.

In sum, the relentless pursuit of military innovation and technological advancement has positioned Gulf armies as formidable and adaptive military forces equipped with cutting-edge capabilities to defend their territories, safeguard their interests, and contribute to regional stability and security. By embracing the transformative potential of advanced technologies, Gulf states have enhanced their military capabilities and reinforced their deterrence posture, resilience, and readiness to respond to a wide range of security challenges, both now and in the future.

C. CHALLENGES AND OPPORTUNITIES IN ADOPTING ADVANCED TECHNOLOGICAL SOLUTIONS

I. **Risk Management and Decision-Making:**
1. Strategic Alignment: Gulf armies must align their technological investments with national security priorities and strategic objectives to allocate resources effectively. Adopting a risk-based approach to decision-making can help identify potential challenges and uncertainties associated with technological adoption, enabling informed choices that maximize operational benefits while mitigating risks.
2. Cost-Benefit Analysis: Conducting comprehensive cost-benefit analyses before investing in advanced technologies is essential to assess the long-term viability and returns on investment. To inform decision-making and resource allocation, gulf countries should consider factors such as lifecycle costs, operational sustainability, and potential risks.

3. Innovation Ecosystem: Fostering an innovation ecosystem that encourages collaboration between defense industry stakeholders, academia, and government entities can accelerate technological advancements and facilitate knowledge sharing. By promoting research and development initiatives, Gulf countries can cultivate a culture of innovation that drives continuous improvement in military capabilities.
4. Adaptive Resilience: Developing adaptive resilience strategies that enable Gulf armies to respond effectively to dynamic threats and technological disruptions. Embracing flexibility and agility in organizational structures and operational processes can enhance readiness and preparedness for unforeseen challenges, ensuring that technological advancements are leveraged to their full potential.
5. Risk Mitigation Measures: Implementing risk mitigation measures, such as contingency planning, redundancy systems, and supply chain diversification, to reduce vulnerabilities and enhance resilience in the face of potential technological failures or disruptions. Gulf countries should prioritize proactive risk management strategies that anticipate and address potential threats to critical military infrastructure and capabilities.

II. **Ethical and Legal Considerations:**
1. Ethical Frameworks: Establishing ethical guidelines and frameworks for the responsible development and use of advanced technologies in military operations. Gulf countries should uphold ethical standards that prioritize human rights, compliance with international law, and transparency in decision-making processes related to the deployment of cutting-edge military capabilities.

2. Legal Compliance: Ensuring compliance with international legal norms and agreements governing the use of advanced technologies in warfare. Gulf armies must adhere to conventions such as the Geneva Conventions and the laws of armed conflict to mitigate potential ethical dilemmas and adhere to principles of proportionality and distinction in using force.
3. Accountability Mechanisms: Implementing accountability mechanisms that promote transparency and oversight in deploying advanced military technologies. Gulf countries should establish mechanisms for evaluating the ethical implications of technological advancements, conducting ethical impact assessments, and holding responsible parties accountable for ethical misconduct in military operations.
4. Public Engagement: Engaging with civil society, academic institutions, and the public to foster dialogue on the ethical implications of technological modernization in defense. Gulf countries should strive to increase public awareness and understanding of advanced military technologies' ethical considerations, promoting public discourse and input in shaping ethical guidelines and policies.
5. International Cooperation: Collaborating with international partners and multilateral organizations to address ethical and legal challenges associated with the use of advanced technologies in military operations. Gulf countries should seek to harmonize ethical standards and legal frameworks with global norms to ensure responsible and ethical use of cutting-edge military capabilities in regional security contexts.

III. **Future Trends and Implications:**

1. Technological Convergence: The convergence of technologies such as artificial intelligence, robotics, and cyber capabilities is reshaping the future battlefield, presenting both opportunities and challenges for Gulf armies. Embracing interdisciplinary approaches and integrated solutions can enhance operational capabilities and strategic outcomes in an increasingly complex and interconnected security environment.
2. Quantum Technologies: The emergence of quantum technologies, including quantum computing and cryptography, has the potential to revolutionize military operations and intelligence capabilities. Gulf countries should invest in research and development initiatives to leverage quantum technologies to enhance cybersecurity, communications, and strategic decision-making in defense.
3. Unmanned Systems: The proliferation of unmanned aerial, ground, and maritime systems is transforming the nature of warfare and reconnaissance missions in the Gulf region. Integrating unmanned systems into military operations can enhance situational awareness, operational flexibility, and precision strike capabilities, providing Gulf armies with a competitive edge in asymmetric and conventional conflicts.
4. Human-Machine Collaboration: Integrating human-machine interfaces and autonomous systems in military operations is blurring the lines between human decision-making and technological automation. Gulf countries must prioritize training and education programs that prepare military personnel to effectively collaborate with autonomous systems and leverage

AI-driven capabilities in complex operational environments.

5. Strategic Adaptation: Embracing strategic adaptation and organizational change to respond proactively to emerging technological trends and geopolitical developments. Gulf armies should cultivate a culture of innovation, adaptability, and strategic foresight to anticipate future challenges and opportunities, fostering resilience and competitiveness in an era of rapid technological change and strategic uncertainty.

This extended chapter offers an in-depth exploration of the multifaceted challenges and opportunities associated with adopting advanced technological solutions in Gulf armies, emphasizing the importance of strategic foresight, risk management, ethical considerations, and innovative approaches in leveraging cutting-edge technologies for enhancing regional security and military capabilities.

IN A NUTSHELL

Integration of Cutting-Edge Technology in Gulf Military Operations

Gulf states have actively integrated advanced technologies into their military operations, significantly enhancing their operational capabilities. This integration spans various domains, including air, land, sea, and cyber. For instance, the UAE's ambitious program in combat robotics exemplifies the strategic incorporation of artificial intelligence and autonomous systems into their military operations. These technologies are not just supplementary; they are central to the operational strategies of Gulf militaries, enabling more effective and efficient mission execution.

Saudi Arabia and the UAE have also focused on enhancing their air and missile defense systems. Saudi Arabia's acquisition of the M-SAM system from South Korea is a testament to its efforts to integrate more sophisticated air defense technologies. Similarly, the UAE has proactively deployed advanced radar and missile systems to bolster its defensive and offensive capabilities.

Innovations Impacting the Efficiency of Gulf Armies

Several key innovations have significantly boosted the efficiency of Gulf armies. One of the most impactful is the use of AI and autonomous systems. For example, Task Force 59, a U.S. Navy unit based in the Gulf, utilizes unmanned surface vessels (USVs) equipped with AI to enhance maritime security and operational efficiency. These systems enable persistent surveillance and reconnaissance without risking human lives, thereby increasing operational tempo and safety.

Another innovation is integrating advanced communication and data-link systems, which ensure that Gulf militaries can maintain robust command and control capabilities even in contested environments. Using satellite communications and advanced networking technologies supports real-time data sharing and decision-making, which is crucial for modern military operations.

Challenges and Opportunities in Adopting Advanced Technological Solutions

While adopting advanced technologies offers significant advantages, it also presents several challenges. One major challenge is the integration of these new technologies into existing military structures and systems. Ensuring compatibility and interoperability between different systems and platforms can be complex and resource-intensive.

Another challenge is the training and development of personnel to operate and maintain these advanced systems effectively. Continuous education and training programs are needed to ensure that military personnel are equipped with the necessary skills and knowledge to leverage these technologies effectively.

However, these challenges also present opportunities. For instance, the drive towards technological integration has spurred innovation within the domestic defense industries of Gulf states. Saudi Arabia's Vision 2030, which includes goals for localizing a significant portion of its military manufacturing, exemplifies this opportunity. By developing local expertise and capabilities, Gulf states can reduce their dependence on foreign technology and improve their self-sufficiency in defense.

Moreover, the focus on advanced technologies like AI and robotics positions Gulf states as leaders in military innovation, potentially opening up new economic avenues related to defense technology exports and collaborations.

In conclusion, the integration of cutting-edge technology has transformed the military capabilities of Gulf states, making them more efficient and effective. While challenges in adoption and integration persist, the strategic opportunities they present can further enhance the Gulf states' positions as modern military powers in the global arena.

Sources and References

[1] https://www.csis.org/analysis/arab-gulf-states-and-iran-military-spending-modernization-and-shifting-military-balance

[2] https://www.reddit.com/r/WarCollege/comments/sqdtcq/how_has_military_technology_improved_since_the/

[3] https://impact.economist.com/perspectives/sites/default/files/eiu_bahrain_edb_report.pdf

[4] https://www.diacc.ae/ai-and-autonomous-defense-transforming-the-arabian-gulf/

[5] https://10xds.com/blog/digital-transformation-challenges-in-uae/

[6] https://www.linkedin.com/pulse/spotlight-ai-military-industry-jean-ko%C3%AFvogui

[7] https://www.mckinsey.com/capabilities/mckinsey-digital/our-insights/the-state-of-ai-in-gcc-countries-and-how-to-overcome-adoption-challenges

[8] https://defenceagenda.com/uaes-ambitious-program/

[9] https://www.defsecme.com/analysis/ai-and-autonomous-defence-transforming-the-arabian-gulf

[10] https://www.usni.org/magazines/proceedings/2021/march/chinas-desert-storm-education

[11] https://www.militaryaerospace.com/communications/article/16709135/us-commanders-assess-technological-lessons-learned-of-gulf-war-ii

[12] https://www.forbes.com/sites/forbestechcouncil/2023/04/17/digital-transformation-in-the-middle-east-challenges-and-opportunities/?sh=58d3d8985b34

[13] https://ciaotest.cc.columbia.edu/olj/sa/sa_99anv02.html

[14] https://sgp.fas.org/crs/natsec/R46458.pdf

[15] https://www.airuniversity.af.edu/Portals/10/ASPJ/journals/Chronicles/nunes.pdf

[16] https://defensescoop.com/2023/05/10/how-us-central-commands-task-forces-are-shaping-the-future-of-operational-ai/

[17] https://academic.oup.com/ia/article/95/4/765/5513164

[18] https://www.ausa.org/news/ai-robotics-could-%E2%80%98change-character-war%E2%80%99

[19] https://www.defense.gov/News/News-Stories/Article/Article/3532946/dod-harnessing-emerging-tech-to-maintain-enduring-advantage/

[20] https://www.health.mil/News/Articles/2021/08/09/Since-Gulf-War-Advanced-Prosthetic-Technology-Saves-Lives-Careers

VIII

Regional Alliances and Partnerships

In exploring the dynamics of regional alliances and partnerships among Gulf states, it is paramount to delve into the intricate web of relationships that shape security dynamics in the region. The Gulf Cooperation Council (GCC) stands as a prominent example of regional collaboration. Founded in 1981 to promote economic, political, and security cooperation among member states, the GCC has played a significant role in fostering joint initiatives such as the Peninsula Shield Force, a collective defense mechanism intended to respond to external aggression and threats to regional stability.

Beyond the GCC, Gulf states have engaged in various bilateral and multilateral partnerships with external actors to enhance their military capabilities further. The United States, in particular, has established extensive defense relationships with Gulf countries, providing advanced military equipment, training, and strategic support to address common security challenges in the region. Additionally, Gulf states have forged partnerships with other international actors, such as the United Kingdom, France, and Russia, to diversify their military support and expertise sources.

The evolving security landscape in the Gulf region has necessitated greater cooperation among states to confront shared threats, such as terrorism, extremism, and maritime security challenges. The Saudi-led coalition in Yemen illustrates the complexity of military alliances in the region, with participating countries coordinating air strikes, intelligence sharing, and logistical support in the conflict against Houthi rebels. While this coalition has faced criticism for civilian casualties and human rights violations, it underscores the strategic imperative for Gulf states to work together to address regional instability.

Despite regional cooperation's benefits, challenges persist in achieving seamless integration and optimal coordination among Gulf states. Differences in strategic priorities, varying military capabilities, and historical animosities can impede the effectiveness of joint initiatives and military operations. Building trust, enhancing communication channels, and aligning national interests are essential steps toward overcoming these obstacles and maximizing the effectiveness of regional partnerships.

The future of Gulf states' military alliances and partnerships will be shaped by evolving security threats, shifting geopolitical dynamics, and changing defense priorities. As Gulf countries navigate these complexities, the strategic value of regional cooperation in enhancing military efficiency and fostering collective security remains paramount in safeguarding the stability and prosperity of the Gulf region.

In recent years, the Gulf region has witnessed a proliferation of non-state actors and hybrid threats that pose significant challenges to traditional security frameworks. Groups like ISIS and other extremist organizations have exploited power vacuums and sectarian tensions to destabilize the region, necessitating a coordinated response from Gulf states. The rise of cyber warfare and weaponized information campaigns further underscores the need for enhanced cooperation in securing critical infrastructure and combating online threats.

Moreover, external powers such as Iran, Turkey, and various global actors have increasingly sought to influence regional dynamics, further complicating the security landscape for Gulf states. Iran's support for proxy groups and its ballistic missile program pose a direct threat to Gulf security, prompting Gulf countries to bolster their defense capabilities and seek closer ties with like-minded allies. Similarly, Turkey's intervention in regional conflicts and its territorial ambitions have raised concerns among Gulf states, leading to calls for greater vigilance and cooperation to counter external meddling.

In response to these multifaceted challenges, Gulf states have pursued a mix of traditional security measures and innovative approaches to enhance their resilience and deterrence capabilities. Investments in state-of-the-art military hardware, intelligence-sharing agreements, joint military exercises, and counter-terrorism initiatives have become integral components of Gulf states' security strategies. The establishment of regional security forums, such as the Riyadh-based Islamic Military Counter Terrorism Coalition (IMCTC), reflects a growing commitment to collective action in addressing shared security threats and promoting stability in the region.

As Gulf states navigate the complexities of a rapidly evolving security environment, the imperative for effective regional alliances and partnerships becomes increasingly apparent. By fostering greater cooperation, coordination, and information-sharing mechanisms, Gulf countries can enhance their collective security posture, deter external threats, and preserve the peace and stability of the region. The path forward lies in deepening existing partnerships, adapting to emerging challenges, and reinforcing a unified front in the face of evolving security risks.

A. ANALYSIS OF GULF STATES' MILITARY ALLIANCES AND PARTNERSHIPS

A closer examination of the intricate tapestry of Gulf states' military alliances and partnerships reveals the multifaceted array of interconnections that underpin regional security dynamics. These alliances, ranging from formal defense pacts to strategic partnerships with global powers, are instrumental in shaping Gulf armies' operational capacities and strategic orientations. By delving deeper into the intricate web of relationships, we can unravel the complexities of security cooperation in the Gulf region and shed light on their implications for regional stability.

Gulf states have cultivated a diverse portfolio of military alliances with both regional and international actors, each serving a unique purpose in bolstering defense capabilities and addressing shared security challenges. The Gulf Cooperation Council (GCC) stands as a cornerstone of regional security architecture, providing a platform for member states to coordinate on defense matters and collaborate on joint military exercises. The GCC's collective security framework fosters a unified front against external threats and promotes intra-regional military cooperation.

At the same time, Gulf states have strategically forged alliances with global powers such as the United States, the United Kingdom, and France, leveraging these partnerships to enhance military capabilities, receive advanced training, and access cutting-edge technology. Through defense cooperation agreements and arms sales, Gulf states have bolstered their defense arsenals and cultivated interoperability with their Western allies, reinforcing their deterrence posture in a volatile security environment.

Beyond formal alliances, Gulf states have also cultivated strategic partnerships with key regional players, such as Egypt, Jordan, and Pakistan, to broaden their strategic reach and enhance their regional influence. These partnerships encompass various dimensions of security cooperation, including intelligence-sharing, counterterrorism efforts, and joint military operations, underscoring the depth of Gulf states' engagement with neighboring countries to address common security challenges.

An in-depth analysis of Gulf states' military alliances reveals a nuanced interplay of motives driving these partnerships, ranging from shared security interests and historical ties to economic imperatives and geopolitical considerations. The historical context of Gulf states' alliances, rooted in the legacy of colonialism, internal rivalries, and regional power dynamics, has shaped the evolution of security partnerships in the region and influenced the strategic calculus of Gulf states in navigating complex security challenges.

Moreover, the geopolitical landscape of the Gulf region, characterized by overlapping security interests, sectarian divides, and external interventions, has necessitated a multifaceted approach to defense cooperation among Gulf states and their allies. The emergence of non-state actors, such as terrorist organizations and insurgent groups, has further underscored the importance of collaborative security efforts and intelligence-sharing mechanisms to counter shared threats and maintain regional stability.

As Gulf states navigate the evolving security dynamics of the region, the recalibration of military alliances and partnerships remains a constant feature of their strategic calculus. Whether in response to emerging security threats, changes in global power dynamics, or internal political shifts, Gulf states must continuously reassess their defense cooperation strategies and adapt to the evolving security landscape to safeguard their national interests and protect regional stability. By closely monitoring these developments and understanding the underlying drivers that shape Gulf states' military alliances, policymakers and analysts can anticipate future trends in regional security cooperation and identify opportunities for enhanced collaboration among stakeholders to address shared security challenges effectively.

B. BENEFITS AND LIMITATIONS OF REGIONAL COOPERATION IN ENHANCING MILITARY EFFICIENCY

Beyond the direct benefits and limitations of military alliances and partnerships among Gulf states, a deeper examination reveals the broader implications and complexities inherent in regional security cooperation. The interconnected nature of global security challenges underscores the significance of collaborative efforts in building a resilient security architecture that can effectively address evolving threats and risks in the Gulf region.

One of the key drivers for increased military cooperation among Gulf states is the shared recognition of common security concerns, including terrorism, cyber threats, and maritime piracy. As non-traditional security threats continue to pose significant challenges to regional stability, joint initiatives to enhance information sharing, intelligence gathering, and capacity-building become essential components of a comprehensive security strategy.

Furthermore, the evolving geopolitical landscape in the Middle East and the strategic competition between regional powers add layers of complexity to military partnerships in the Gulf. The intricate web of alliances, rivalries, and overlapping interests complicates the dynamics of regional security cooperation, requiring careful navigation and diplomatic finesse to maintain a delicate balance between cooperation and competition.

The role of external actors, such as the United States, Russia, and European powers, in shaping military partnerships in the Gulf also merits attention. External support and arms sales to Gulf states can enable and constrain regional security initiatives' autonomy and effectiveness. Balancing the interests of external partners with the imperatives of national security and sovereignty poses a persistent challenge for Gulf states seeking to strengthen their defense capabilities through strategic alliances.

Moreover, the long-term sustainability of military partnerships in the Gulf hinges on the ability of participating states to adapt to changing security dynamics and emerging threats. Investments in technological innovation, defense research and development, and joint training programs are crucial for maintaining military readiness and agility in an increasingly volatile and unpredictable security environment.

A complex web of alliances, rivalries, and overlapping interests among key players characterizes the geopolitical landscape of the Gulf region. The rivalry between Saudi Arabia and Iran, for example, has shaped the security dynamics in the region, with both countries seeking to project influence and assert dominance through various means, including military partnerships and alliances.

Furthermore, the involvement of external actors, such as the United States, Russia, China, and European powers, adds another layer of complexity to the security landscape in the Gulf. These external powers often play a significant role in shaping Gulf states' military partnerships and security arrangements, either through arms sales, training programs, or political alliances. The competition for influence and strategic positioning in the region further complicates the dynamics of security cooperation among Gulf states.

Amid these challenges and complexities, efforts to enhance military interoperability, joint exercises, and defense coordination among Gulf states have gained momentum in recent years. The establishment of the Gulf Cooperation Council (GCC) and initiatives such as the Peninsula Shield Force have aimed to foster greater cooperation and unity among Gulf states in addressing common security threats and challenges.

However, the effectiveness and sustainability of military partnerships in the Gulf will depend on a range of factors, including political will, resource allocation, technological capabilities, and the ability to adapt to evolving security dynamics. Building strong and resilient military partnerships will promote stability, security, and prosperity in the Gulf as the region continues to navigate complex geopolitical challenges and threats.

C. CASE STUDIES HIGHLIGHTING SUCCESSFUL COLLABORATIVE EFFORTS IN THE REGION

Working together, Gulf states significantly boost regional security and tackle shared challenges. This section examines successful military collaboration in the Gulf area, highlighting the advantages and lessons learned from these joint efforts.

Case Study 1: The Peninsula Shield Force

The Peninsula Shield Force, established by the Gulf Cooperation Council (GCC) in 1984, serves as a prime example of successful military collaboration among Gulf states. Comprising troops from member countries, this joint military force was created to respond to regional threats and security challenges, particularly in the aftermath of the Iran-Iraq War. Over the years, the Peninsula Shield Force has conducted numerous training exercises, including joint maneuvers and war games, to enhance interoperability among member states' armed forces. Additionally, the force has been deployed to manage security crises within the Gulf region, showcasing its ability to respond swiftly and effectively to emergent threats. Through the Peninsula Shield Force, Gulf states have demonstrated a collective commitment to regional security and stability, underscoring the importance of solidarity in the face of common challenges.

Case Study 2: Integrated Air and Missile Defense

The integration of air and missile defense systems among Gulf states has emerged as a critical component of regional security architecture. By coordinating their efforts to develop a comprehensive air defense network, Gulf countries have significantly enhanced their ability to detect, track, and neutralize airborne threats, including ballistic missiles and unmanned aerial vehicles. Central to this collaboration is the sharing of intelligence, the deployment of advanced radar systems, and joint training programs that foster high operational readiness. The success of integrated air and missile defense initiatives underscores the significance of mutual trust and cooperation in safeguarding Gulf airspace against potential security risks.

Case Study 3: Maritime Security Partnerships

Maritime security partnerships among Gulf states have played a vital role in enhancing the safety and stability of regional waters. Given the strategic importance of maritime trade routes in the Gulf, cooperation in this domain has been instrumental in countering maritime threats such as piracy, smuggling, and trafficking. Collaborative initiatives, such as joint patrols, information-sharing mechanisms, and capacity-building programs, have bolstered the capabilities of Gulf navies to monitor and secure vital sea lanes. Furthermore, joint naval exercises and coordinated responses to maritime incidents have demonstrated the collective resolve of Gulf countries to maintain a secure maritime environment that facilitates economic activity and prevents transnational threats.

Case Study 4: Cybersecurity Cooperation The proliferation of cyber threats has necessitated greater cooperation among Gulf states in cybersecurity. Recognizing the interconnected nature of cyberspace and the vulnerabilities inherent in digital infrastructure, Gulf nations have intensified their efforts to strengthen cybersecurity measures through collaborative initiatives. These efforts include sharing threat intelligence, establishing joint cybersecurity task forces, and the development of cyber defense strategies that prioritize information sharing and incident response coordination. By pooling their resources and expertise in cybersecurity, Gulf states have bolstered their resilience against cyber attacks, safeguarding critical systems and data from malicious actors seeking to disrupt regional stability and security.

Conclusion

The case studies presented in this section illustrate the multifaceted benefits of military collaboration among Gulf states in enhancing regional security and resilience. From the formation of the Peninsula Shield Force to the integration of air and missile defense systems, and the cooperation in maritime security and cybersecurity domains, Gulf countries have demonstrated their capacity to address shared security challenges through collective action. The success of these collaborative efforts highlights the importance of trust, communication, and solidarity among Gulf states in safeguarding the region against evolving threats and promoting stability and peace in the Gulf.

IN A NUTSHELL

> **Analysis of Gulf States' Military Alliances and Partnerships**
>
> The Gulf Cooperation Council (GCC) states—Saudi Arabia, Kuwait, the United Arab Emirates, Qatar, Bahrain, and Oman—have developed a complex network of military alliances and partnerships, primarily driven by the need to address regional security threats and balance external influences. The United States has been a pivotal military partner for the GCC, providing advanced weapons systems, training, and defense infrastructure support. This relationship, however, has seen fluctuations

due to varying U.S. policy stances and Gulf states' increasing desire for strategic autonomy.

In recent years, there has been a noticeable shift as Gulf states seek to diversify their military partnerships beyond traditional allies like the U.S. For instance, Saudi Arabia and the UAE have expanded their military relationships with China and Russia, partly driven by U.S. hesitancy to fully support their regional activities, such as the war in Yemen. This diversification strategy also includes enhancing regional military cooperation among GCC members, although this has been challenged by internal disputes, such as the Qatar blockade which was resolved in January 2021.

Benefits and Limitations of Regional Cooperation in Enhancing Military Efficiency

Benefits
Regional cooperation among the GCC states offers several benefits that enhance military efficiency:
Interoperability: Joint military exercises and equipment standardization foster interoperability among GCC militaries, facilitating more effective collective defense operations.
Strategic Deterrence: A unified regional military stance enhances the GCC's ability to act as a strategic deterrent against common threats, such as Iran's regional influence.
- Cost-Effectiveness: Collaborative defense procurement and shared development of military technology can reduce costs and increase bargaining power on the international stage.

Limitations
However, regional cooperation faces significant limitations:

- Political Disparities: Internal political disputes among GCC members, as evidenced by the Qatar blockade, can undermine trust and cooperation.
   - Varying Defense Priorities: Different threat perceptions and defense priorities among GCC states complicate the development of a cohesive military strategy.
   - Dependency on External Powers: Heavy reliance on non-regional powers like the U.S. for military technology and support can limit the depth of regional military integration.

Case Studies Highlighting Successful Collaborative Efforts in the Region

Peninsula Shield Force
The Peninsula Shield Force, established in 1984, is the GCC's joint military venture. It was notably deployed in Bahrain in 2011 to protect government infrastructure during the Arab Spring protests. This deployment underscored the potential for GCC military collaboration in responding to internal security threats.

Environmental and Security Collaboration
Recent environmental collaborations, such as those initiated around the COP28 discussions, demonstrate a newer form of security cooperation that addresses non-traditional security threats like climate change. These efforts are particularly significant as they build trust and open channels for more traditional security dialogues.

U.S.-GCC Defense Integration
The U.S. and GCC states have worked on integrating their defense systems to enhance regional security architectures. This

integration supports the GCC's defense capabilities against asymmetric threats and contributes to broader regional stability, benefiting both Gulf security and broader U.S. strategic interests in the Middle East.

In conclusion, while the GCC states have made significant strides in developing their military alliances and regional cooperation frameworks, challenges remain. Overcoming internal divisions and reducing dependency on external powers are crucial for the future effectiveness and sustainability of these cooperative efforts. The strategic value of such regional cooperation continues to be critical for the security and stability of the Gulf region.

Sources and references

[1] https://academic.oup.com/book/39793/chapter-abstract/339893654?redirectedFrom=fulltext

[2] https://gulfif.org/uniting-the-gulf-regional-collaboration-at-cop28-for-climate-change/

[3] https://www.ispionline.it/en/publication/defense-integration-refashions-the-us-gcc-alliance-118338

[4] https://www.wilsoncenter.org/article/americas-key-gulf-arab-partners-embrace-non-alignment-tilt-toward-china

[5] https://www.atlanticcouncil.org/blogs/menasource/the-way-for-the-us-to-ensure-gulf-security-is-through-partnership-not-policing/

[6] https://www.britannica.com/topic/Gulf-Cooperation-Council

[7] https://www.csis.org/analysis/unique-promise-environmental-cooperation-gulf

[8] https://carnegie-mec.org/2023/10/30/future-of-gulf-cooperation-council-amid-saudi-emirati-rivalry-pub-90867

[9] https://www.unitar.org/about/news-stories/news/successful-partnership-between-unitar-and-gulf-cooperation-council-2016

[10] https://www.csis.org/analysis/solving-europes-defense-dilemma-overcoming-challenges-european-defense-cooperation

[11] https://www.csis.org/analysis/changing-trends-gulf-military-and-security-forces-net-assessment

[12] https://www.mea.gov.in/Portal/ForeignRelation/Gulf_Cooperation_Council_MEA_Website.pdf

[13] https://journals.sagepub.com/doi/full/10.1177/23477989211057341

[14] https://2009-2017.state.gov/t/pm/rls/rpt/fmtrpt/2001/2568.htm

[15] https://www.unescap.org/sites/default/files/ch2_0.pdf
[16] https://www.sipri.org/sites/default/files/YB06ch04.pdf
[17] https://www.gcc-sg.org/en-us/MediaCenter/NewsCooperation/News/Pages/news2021-7-5-2.aspx
[18] https://www.frstrategie.org/en/publications/defense-et-industries/defence-acquisition-cooperation-benefits-2016
[19] https://apps.dtic.mil/sti/citations/AD1065358

IX

Crisis Management and Conflict Resolution

Strategies for effective crisis management within Gulf armies require a multifaceted approach encompassing preparedness, communication, decision-making, and coordination. In times of crisis, swift and decisive action is essential to mitigate risks and safeguard national interests. Gulf armies must prioritize training programs that simulate crisis scenarios and test responses in real-time to enhance readiness and resilience.

Furthermore, establishing clear command structures and communication channels is crucial for effective crisis management. Prompt and accurate dissemination of information among military leaders and personnel is paramount to coordinate operations and make informed decisions. Regular drills and exercises that involve scenario-based training can help improve communication flows and promote a coordinated response to unforeseen events.

In the context of conflict resolution, Gulf armies must be adept at employing diplomatic measures to de-escalate tensions and negotiate peaceful resolutions. Building strong diplomatic ties with neighboring countries and regional actors can facilitate dialogue and cooperation in addressing shared security challenges. Additionally, leveraging international partnerships and engaging in multilateral forums can provide avenues for conflict mediation and resolution.

Lessons learned from past crises and conflicts should inform future crisis management and resolution strategies. Analyzing successful interventions and identifying areas for improvement can help Gulf armies enhance their capabilities and effectiveness in addressing security threats. By adopting a proactive and holistic approach to crisis management and conflict resolution, Gulf armies can better safeguard the stability and security of the region.

Moreover, enhancing intelligence gathering and analysis capabilities is crucial for anticipating and responding to potential threats. Gulf armies should invest in advanced technology and surveillance systems to monitor activities in the region and identify emerging security risks. Additionally, collaboration with intelligence agencies and sharing information with regional partners can enhance situational awareness and support timely decision-making during crises.

Effective crisis management also requires the establishment of clear protocols for coordination and cooperation with other branches of the military, government agencies, and international partners. Integrated command structures and joint training exercises can facilitate seamless communication and interoperability among different entities involved in crisis response efforts.

Furthermore, investing in humanitarian assistance and disaster relief capabilities can enhance Gulf armies' ability to provide critical support to affected populations during crises. Building relationships with civilian organizations and nongovernmental agencies can facilitate swift and coordinated humanitarian responses in times of need, ensuring the well-being of impacted communities.

Additionally, emphasizing strategic communication during crises is vital for maintaining public trust and transparency. Gulf armies should have robust communication strategies in place to provide timely updates, address concerns, and rally public support for crisis response efforts. Engaging with the media and leveraging social media platforms can help disseminate accurate information and counter misinformation, ensuring a cohesive and united response to crises.

In conclusion, a comprehensive approach to crisis management within Gulf armies should encompass training, communication, diplomacy, intelligence gathering, coordination, humanitarian assistance, and strategic communication. By integrating these elements into their strategic planning and operational procedures, Gulf armies can effectively mitigate security risks, resolve conflicts, and maintain regional stability.

A. STRATEGIES FOR EFFECTIVE CRISIS MANAGEMENT WITHIN GULF ARMIES

In times of crisis, the ability of Gulf armies to effectively manage and respond to challenges is crucial for maintaining national security and stability. This chapter delves into the strategies Gulf states employ to navigate crises and mitigate potential threats to their interests.

One key strategy revolves around proactive planning and preparedness. Gulf armies often engage in scenario-based training exercises and simulations to simulate different crises and develop response mechanisms. These armies can enhance their readiness to address crises effectively by identifying potential risks and vulnerabilities. These preparedness efforts include ensuring sufficient stockpiles of resources such as food, water, medical supplies, and fuel to sustain operations during extended crises.

Furthermore, effective crisis management within Gulf armies involves clear communication and coordination among different military branches and with relevant government agencies. Establishing a well-defined chain of command and communication protocols ensures swift and effective decision-making during times of crisis. Regular drills and exercises play a crucial role in testing the efficacy of these communication systems and ensuring seamless coordination in high-pressure situations.

Another critical aspect of crisis management is deploying specialized crisis response teams. These teams are trained to respond rapidly to emergent situations involving natural disasters, internal unrest, or external threats. Specialized training programs equip these teams with the necessary skills and resources to handle various crisis scenarios, from medical emergencies to hostage situations or terrorist attacks.

Additionally, leveraging technology and intelligence capabilities is essential for effective crisis management. Gulf states invest heavily in surveillance systems, drones, and other advanced technologies to enhance situational awareness and intelligence gathering. By utilizing sophisticated monitoring tools and data analytics, Gulf armies can anticipate threats, identify trends, and respond quickly to rapidly evolving crises.

Furthermore, building resilience and adaptability into crisis management strategies is crucial for handling unforeseen challenges.

Gulf armies continually review and update their crisis response plans based on lessons learned from past experiences and emerging threats. Flexibility in decision-making and the ability to adjust real-time tactics are essential for effectively managing crises in dynamic and unpredictable environments.

Lastly, forging strong regional partnerships and alliances is a cornerstone of Gulf states' crisis management approach. By collaborating with neighboring countries, regional organizations, and international partners, Gulf armies can tap into additional resources, expertise, and information-sharing networks to address complex and transnational crises effectively. Multilateral cooperation enhances collective security and fosters a unified response to common threats that may transcend individual national borders.

Ultimately, an integrated and multifaceted approach that encompasses proactive planning, effective communication, specialized response capabilities, technological innovation, adaptability, and regional cooperation is essential for Gulf armies to navigate crises successfully and safeguard national security in the face of evolving challenges.

B. APPROACHES TO RESOLVING CONFLICTS AND MAINTAINING REGIONAL STABILITY

The quest for regional stability in the Gulf states remains a complex challenge that demands a multifaceted approach to conflict resolution. The historical backdrop of the Middle East, marked by longstanding rivalries and power struggles, underscores the urgency of fostering peaceful coexistence among Gulf countries. In this context, it is imperative to delve deeper into the various strategies and mechanisms that can be leveraged to address conflicts and promote sustainable stability in the region.

Diplomatic negotiations and dialogue stand out as indispensable tools in the arsenal of conflict resolution. The art of diplomacy, characterized by nuanced communication and negotiation skills, holds the potential to de-escalate tensions and pave the way for constructive dialogue. Gulf states can harness diplomatic channels to directly talk with conflicting parties, leveraging their influence to bridge divides and find common ground. Moreover, multilateral platforms such as the United Nations, Arab League, and Gulf Cooperation Council offer valuable arenas for facilitating dialogue and consensus-building among regional actors.

In the realm of confidence-building measures, cultivating mutual trust and transparency emerges as a linchpin of conflict prevention. By fostering open communication and cooperation on security issues, Gulf states can mitigate the risk of misperceptions and miscalculations that often fuel conflicts. Confidence-building measures encompass a spectrum of initiatives, including military-to-military dialogues, joint exercises, and trust-building measures to enhance communication channels and reduce the likelihood of conflict escalation.

The deployment of conflict resolution mechanisms, such as mediation and arbitration, represents an additional layer of engagement in addressing regional disputes. Third-party intervention by impartial mediators or arbitrators can offer a neutral platform for disputing parties to explore peaceful settlements, drawing upon diplomatic finesse and conflict resolution expertise to navigate complex negotiations. Whether facilitated by regional actors or international organizations, mediation efforts hold the promise of unlocking stalemates, fostering compromise, and charting a path towards sustainable peace.

Economic interdependence and cooperation serve as pillars of regional stability, underscoring the interconnected nature of security and prosperity in the Gulf states. By forging economic partnerships, trade agreements, and investment ties, countries in the region can cultivate shared interests that incentivize collaboration and deter conflict. The economic dimension of regional integration bolsters economic resilience and fosters a sense of interdependence that underscores the high costs of instability and the dividends of peaceful coexistence.

Beyond diplomacy and economics, conflict prevention looms large on the agenda of regional stability. Building institutional capacities for conflict analysis, early warning systems, and peacebuilding initiatives equips Gulf states with the tools to proactively anticipate and manage potential crises. By investing in preventive diplomacy and strategic foresight, countries in the region can avert conflicts before they escalate, bolstering resilience and laying the groundwork for enduring peace.

In conclusion, pursuing regional stability in the Gulf states demands a comprehensive approach integrating diplomatic dialogue, confidence-building measures, conflict resolution mechanisms, economic cooperation, and conflict prevention strategies. This multifaceted toolkit underscores the region's interconnected nature of security challenges, mandating a collective commitment to dialogue, cooperation, and peacemaking. As Gulf states navigate the complex landscape of regional dynamics, cultivating a culture of peace and cooperation stands as a beacon of hope for a future characterized by stability, prosperity, and harmony in the Gulf region.

C. LESSONS LEARNED FROM PAST CONFLICTS AND IMPLICATIONS FOR FUTURE ENGAGEMENTS

Throughout history, Gulf states and their armies have navigated a complex landscape of conflicts, leaving indelible marks on their military strategies and operational capabilities. Drawing upon these experiences offers valuable insights that can shape future engagements' direction and enhance their forces' readiness. By delving deeper into the lessons learned from past conflicts, decision-makers can glean a more nuanced understanding of navigating the challenges ahead effectively.

One pivotal lesson that has emerged from past conflicts is the critical importance of unity and cohesion among military forces. In many historical engagements, Gulf armies faced challenges stemming from a lack of synergy between different military branches. This lack of coordination often led to disjointed operations and hindered the overall effectiveness of the forces. To address this, military leaders must prioritize joint training exercises and foster a culture of collaboration among all branches of the armed forces. By promoting interoperability and communication, Gulf states can ensure that their military units work seamlessly together, thereby enhancing their operational effectiveness on the battlefield.

Moreover, a deeper examination of past conflicts underscores the necessity of strategic flexibility in military operations. In dynamic and unpredictable environments, rigid doctrines and inflexible strategies can prove to be detrimental to achieving mission success. Gulf armies must be willing to adapt and innovate in response to evolving threats and changing circumstances. By cultivating a culture of agility and empowering commanders to make timely and informed decisions, military forces can better respond to the fluid nature of modern warfare and maintain a competitive edge over adversaries.

Furthermore, the lessons learned from past conflicts highlight the pivotal role of technology and intelligence capabilities in shaping military outcomes. Gulf states have recognized the strategic advantage of advancements in military technology, such as drones, cyber capabilities, and precision-guided munitions. By leveraging these tools effectively, armies can bolster their situational awareness, improve target accuracy, and enhance overall battlefield dominance. Investing in cutting-edge technologies and fostering a robust intelligence infrastructure will be essential for Gulf states to stay ahead of emerging threats and challenges in future engagements.

Additionally, the professional development of military personnel emerges as a cornerstone of success in past conflicts. Well-trained and motivated troops are the backbone of any effective military operation. Gulf armies must prioritize continuous training and education programs to ensure their personnel have the skills and expertise to excel in high-pressure situations. By investing in leadership development, morale-building initiatives, and mental resilience training, military forces can enhance their overall readiness and capacity to respond to the demands of modern warfare.

In conclusion, a deeper exploration of the lessons learned from past conflicts underscores the imperative for Gulf states to embrace unity, flexibility, technological innovation, and personnel development as foundational pillars of their military readiness. By integrating these insights into their strategic planning and operational paradigms, decision-makers can proactively prepare their forces to navigate the uncertainties of future engagements and uphold regional security with vigilance and efficacy.

IN A NUTSHELL

Strategies for Effective Crisis Management within Gulf Armies

Effective crisis management within Gulf armies necessitates a comprehensive approach integrating preparedness, robust communication systems, informed decision-making, and seamless coordination. The primary strategy involves the development of advanced simulation and training programs replicating potential crisis scenarios. These programs should focus on enhancing the decision-making capabilities of officers under stress and improving the operational readiness of the troops. Additionally, establishing a centralized command and control center that leverages real-time intelligence and data analytics can significantly enhance situational awareness and response times.

Approaches to Resolving Conflicts and Maintaining Regional Stability

Maintaining regional stability in the Gulf requires diplomatic finesse and strategic military preparedness. One effective approach is enhancing multilateral security frameworks that encourage cooperation and dialogue among Gulf states and other regional actors. Learning from the ASEAN model, Gulf states could establish foundational principles such as mutual respect, non-interference, and peaceful dispute resolution to guide their interactions. Furthermore, engaging in regular diplomatic dialogues and joint military exercises with neighboring countries can build trust and reduce misunderstandings that might lead to conflicts.

Lessons Learned from Past Conflicts and Implications for Future Engagements

Past conflicts in the Gulf region offer critical lessons that can shape future military strategies and crisis management approaches. The Iran-Iraq War and the Gulf War highlighted the importance of technological superiority and the need for effective command and control systems. These conflicts also underscored the risks associated with underestimating the enemy and the necessity of maintaining a well-trained and adaptable military force.

From these lessons, Gulf armies can derive several implications for future engagements:

1. **Technological Advancement**: Continued investment in cutting-edge military technology is crucial. This includes cyber capabilities, unmanned systems, and advanced surveillance technologies that can provide significant advantages in future conflicts.

2. **Alliance Building**: Strengthening alliances and international partnerships remains vital. Diversifying military and diplomatic ties can help Gulf states navigate complex geopolitical landscapes and enhance their strategic security.

3. **Civil-Military Relations**: Enhancing the military's professionalization and ensuring it operates under civilian oversight can improve governance and stability within the state, reducing the likelihood of internal conflicts.

In conclusion, Gulf armies must adopt a multifaceted strategy for crisis management that includes advanced training, robust command and control systems, and effective diplomatic engagement. Lessons from past conflicts should guide future military preparations and strategies, ensuring that Gulf states are better prepared to face and resolve crises while maintaining regional stability.

Sources and references

[1] https://carnegieendowment.org/files/CP256_Wehrey-Sokolsky_final.pdf
[2] https://www.cfc.forces.gc.ca/259/260/263/clark2.pdf
[3] https://www.rand.org/content/dam/rand/pubs/research_reports/RRA900/RRA904-1/RAND_RRA904-1.pdf
[4] https://www.tandfonline.com/doi/full/10.1080/03932729.2020.1741268
[5] https://press.un.org/en/2023/sc14548.doc.htm
[6] https://www.rand.org/content/dam/rand/pubs/perspectives/PE300/PE353/RAND_PE353.pdf
[7] https://www.cartercenter.org/resources/pdfs/news/peace_publications/conflict_resolution/Solving_Territorial_Conflicts.pdf
[8] https://apps.dtic.mil/sti/trecms/pdf/AD1164474.pdf
[9] https://carnegieendowment.org/2023/05/03/consolidation-and-fragmentation-in-arab-security-sectors-pub-89526
[10] https://apps.dtic.mil/sti/trecms/pdf/AD1114571.pdf
[11] https://www.sigar.mil/pdf/lessonslearned/SIGAR-21-46-LL.pdf
[12] https://www.esd.whs.mil/Portals/54/Documents/FOID/Reading%20Room/Other/15-F-0901_DOC_01_Dissuasion_Strategy_200612.pdf
[13] https://www.rand.org/pubs/research_briefs/RB9975.html
[14] https://www.armyupress.army.mil/Portals/7/Research%20and%20Books/2024/Feb/Deveraux-Lessons-Learned-2024.pdf
[15] https://2001-2009.state.gov/r/pa/ei/wh/15425.htm
[16] https://apps.dtic.mil/sti/pdfs/ADA256145.pdf
[17] https://unesdoc.unesco.org/ark:/48223/pf0000120112
[18] https://csis-website-prod.s3.amazonaws.com/s3fs-public/160628_Les-

sons_of_the_Gulf_War_1990-1991_full.pdf
[19] https://www.researchgate.net/publication/48327974_Managing_Transboundary_Crises_Identifying_the_Building_Blocks_of_an_Effective_Response_System
[20] https://www.researchgate.net/publication/46540603_The_New_World_of_Crises_and_Crisis_Management_Implications_for_Policymaking_and_Research

X

Future Prospects and Recommendations

Looking ahead, the Gulf states' military landscape will likely witness several key trends shaping their efficiency and capabilities. One of the most notable trends is the continued emphasis on modernization and advanced military technology. Gulf countries are willing to invest in cutting-edge weapons systems, cyber capabilities, and defense infrastructure to enhance their military prowess.

In recent years, Gulf states have increasingly focused on diversifying their defense acquisitions, moving away from reliance on traditional Western suppliers to explore partnerships with emerging defense exporters such as China and Russia. This shift reflects a broader strategy of reducing dependence on any single source of weapons and technology while gaining access to a wider array of defense solutions.

Additionally, the Gulf states will likely focus on improving training programs and personnel capabilities to bolster their operational effectiveness. Investing in human capital and ensuring that military personnel are well-trained and equipped to handle a range of scenarios will be crucial in enhancing overall military readiness. As asymmetric threats evolve, specialized training in counterinsurgency, counterterrorism, and urban warfare will become increasingly important for Gulf armies.

Moreover, regional alliances and partnerships are expected to play a significant role in shaping the future of Gulf armies. Collaborative efforts with neighboring countries and international allies can provide mutual defense benefits, sharing intelligence and resources to address common security challenges effectively. The Gulf Cooperation Council (GCC) has long served as a platform for regional security cooperation, with joint military exercises and intelligence-sharing mechanisms enhancing collective defense capabilities.

In light of these trends, several recommendations can be made further to enhance the efficiency and capabilities of Gulf armies. Firstly, there is a need to prioritize training and professional development investments to ensure that military personnel are adequately prepared for the dynamic and evolving security environment. Continuous education and training programs should be tailored to address emerging threats, equipping personnel with the skills and knowledge to respond effectively.

Secondly, fostering innovation and technological advancements within Gulf armies will be essential to remain competitive and effective in modern warfare. Embracing emerging technologies such as artificial intelligence, unmanned systems, and cyber capabilities can significantly enhance the operational effectiveness of Gulf militaries. Integration of these technologies into existing systems and platforms will be crucial to maintaining a technological edge over potential adversaries.

Lastly, policymakers should continue strengthening regional alliances and partnerships to promote security cooperation and collective defense initiatives. Collaborative efforts can help address common security threats and promote stability in the Gulf region. By enhancing interoperability among Gulf armies and fostering closer ties with international partners, the collective defense posture of Gulf states can be strengthened, ensuring a more coordinated and effective response to security challenges.

By implementing these recommendations and adapting to emerging trends, Gulf states can enhance their military capabilities, boost operational efficiency, and contribute to regional stability and security in the years to come. The evolving landscape of Gulf armies presents challenges and opportunities, with strategic planning and proactive measures crucial to navigating the complexities of modern warfare and defense in the region.

A. ANTICIPATED TRENDS IN GULF ARMIES' EFFICIENCY AND CAPABILITIES

Technological Advancements: Gulf states are at the forefront of adopting cutting-edge military technology to enhance their operational capabilities. Anticipated trends include the integration of artificial intelligence (AI) and machine learning into command and control systems to improve decision-making processes and increase operational efficiency. Unmanned systems, such as drones and autonomous vehicles, are also expected to play a significant role in reconnaissance, surveillance, and target acquisition, allowing Gulf armies to gather real-time intelligence and conduct precision strikes with minimal risk to personnel.

Moreover, developing cyber warfare capabilities is a top priority for Gulf states to safeguard their critical infrastructure and information systems from cyber threats. Investment in offensive and defensive cyber capabilities, including establishing dedicated cyber units and training cyber experts, will enable Gulf armies to conduct cyber operations effectively in support of their military objectives.

Advanced weaponry, including next-generation fighter jets, missile defense systems, and precision-guided munitions, will further enhance the firepower and lethality of Gulf armies. These capabilities will enable Gulf states to project power and deter potential adversaries while maintaining a technological edge in the region's defense landscape.

Enhanced Training and Personnel Development: Gulf states recognize the importance of investing in their human capital to ensure their military personnel are well-trained, highly skilled, and adaptable to evolving security challenges. Anticipated trends include implementing advanced training programs, simulation technologies, and live-fire exercises to enhance combat readiness and operational effectiveness.

Professional development initiatives, such as leadership training and management courses, will cultivate a cadre of competent leaders capable of making sound decisions under pressure. Interdisciplinary collaboration among different military branches will foster a culture of teamwork and coordination, enabling Gulf armies to operate cohesively in joint and combined operations.

Furthermore, the recruitment and retention of top talent and the promotion of diversity and inclusion within the ranks will strengthen Gulf armies' capabilities and resilience. By investing in their personnel's development, Gulf states can build a highly skilled and motivated workforce capable of effectively meeting modern warfare demands and safeguarding national security interests.

Strategic Partnerships and Alliances: Gulf states leverage strategic partnerships and alliances with regional and international actors to enhance their military capabilities and collective security posture. Anticipated trends include deepening cooperation with like-minded countries, such as the United States, France, and the United Kingdom, through defense agreements, joint military exercises, and technology transfer programs.

Closer collaboration with regional partners, such as the Gulf Cooperation Council (GCC) countries and neighboring states, will strengthen mutual defense cooperation and foster interoperability among Gulf armies. Information-sharing agreements, intelligence cooperation, and joint counterterrorism efforts will enhance the collective ability of Gulf states to respond to shared security threats and promote regional stability.

Moreover, participation in multilateral security frameworks, such as the coalition against terrorism or maritime security initiatives, will enhance Gulf states' influence and presence in regional security architecture. By forging strong partnerships and alliances, Gulf armies can leverage collective capabilities and resources to address complex security challenges and safeguard the Gulf region's stability and prosperity.

Shifts in Defense Posture and Doctrine: Gulf states are re-evaluating their defense postures and military doctrines to adapt to evolving security threats, geopolitical dynamics, and technological advancements. Anticipated trends include a focus on developing asymmetric warfare capabilities to counter unconventional threats, such as terrorism, insurgency, and hybrid warfare tactics.

Rapid response forces, specialized counterterrorism units, and strategic reserves must be prioritized to enhance Gulf armies' agility and flexibility in responding to emergencies and crises. Enhanced integration of air, land, and sea forces and joint and combined operations will strengthen Gulf countries' ability to conduct integrated military campaigns and project power effectively across different domains.

Furthermore, adopting a comprehensive defense strategy encompassing deterrence, defense, and readiness will guide Gulf states in shaping their force structures, modernizing their equipment, and optimizing their operational capabilities. By embracing a forward-looking defense posture and doctrine, Gulf armies can effectively address emerging threats and challenges while safeguarding national security interests and regional stability.

Emphasis on LocalDefense Industry: Gulf states are increasingly prioritizing the development of their local defense industry capabilities to reduce dependence on foreign suppliers and enhance self-reliance in defense production. Anticipated trends include expanding domestic defense manufacturing capabilities, fostering innovation and research and development in defense technology, and promoting local defense industries through investment and policy support.

The establishment of defense industrial complexes, technology parks, and research institutions will stimulate growth in the defense sector and create opportunities for local businesses to participate in defense projects. Collaboration with international defense firms and technology partners will facilitate knowledge transfer, technology exchange, and capacity building to enhance the competitiveness and sophistication of Gulf countries' defense industries.

Promoting local defense production will not only strengthen Gulf states' economic resilience and strategic autonomy but also support national security objectives by increasing domestic availability of cutting-edge defense technologies and equipment. By investing in their defense industry capabilities, Gulf states can enhance their industrial base, create high-tech jobs, and contribute to economic diversification while advancing their military modernization goals.

Regional Security Cooperation: In the face of shared security challenges and regional instabilities, Gulf states are prioritizing regional security cooperation initiatives to strengthen collective defense capabilities and promote stability in the Gulf region. Anticipated trends include fostering closer coordination on maritime security, border protection, intelligence sharing, and joint military exercises to enhance interoperability and readiness among Gulf armies.

Closer collaboration within the GCC framework, as well as with regional partners like Egypt, Jordan, and other Arab states, will strengthen mutual defense cooperation and build trust among Gulf countries. Multilateral security dialogues, peacekeeping operations, and conflict resolution mechanisms will further enhance regional security architecture and promote cooperation in addressing common security threats.

Participation in regional security forums, such as the Manama Dialogue or the Riyadh Summit, will provide platforms for Gulf states to engage in strategic dialogues, exchange perspectives on regional security challenges, and coordinate responses to emerging threats. By fostering regional security cooperation, Gulf armies can build trust, enhance collective capabilities, and contribute to a more stable and secure environment in the Gulf region.

Focus on Non-Traditional Security Challenges: Gulf states increasingly focus on non-traditional security challenges, such as cybersecurity, environmental security, and humanitarian crises, which can impact national security and stability. Anticipated trends include building resilience against cyber threats by developing robust cybersecurity strategies, incident response mechanisms, and information-sharing frameworks to mitigate cyber risks and protect critical infrastructure.

Addressing environmental security risks, including climate change impacts, water scarcity, and natural disasters, will require Gulf states to incorporate climate resilience and sustainability considerations into their defense planning and operations. Anticipated trends include the development of green technologies, renewable energy solutions, and environmental management practices to reduce the ecological footprint of military activities and enhance environmental stewardship.

Moreover, enhancing disaster response capabilities, conducting humanitarian assistance and disaster relief operations, and collaborating with international organizations and civil society partners will enable Gulf states to respond effectively to humanitarian crises and emergencies within and beyond their borders. Building resilience against non-traditional security challenges will bolster Gulf armies' preparedness and adaptive capacity to address complex and interrelated threats while safeguarding national security interests and promoting regional stability.

By proactively addressing these anticipated trends and challenges, Gulf armies can enhance their efficiency, capabilities, and readiness to effectively navigate the evolving security landscape of the Gulf region while safeguarding peace, stability, and prosperity for their nations and people.

B. RECOMMENDATIONS FOR ENHANCING OPERATIONAL EFFECTIVENESS AND AUTONOMY

As Gulf states navigate the evolving security landscape characterized by a myriad of challenges ranging from regional conflicts to asymmetric threats, the imperative to enhance operational effectiveness and bolster military autonomy remains paramount. In the pursuit of these strategic goals, a nuanced and multifaceted approach is essential to address the complexities of modern warfare and ensure a robust defense posture.

1. Foster LocalDefense Industries: The cultivation of local defense industries represents a strategic imperative for Gulf states seeking to reduce their reliance on foreign suppliers and enhance their self-sufficiency in defense production. By investing in research and development capabilities, promoting collaboration between academia and industry, and incentivizing domestic manufacturing, Gulf states can bolster their economic resilience and strengthen their defense industrial base. The establishment of specialized defense research centers, technology parks, and innovation hubs can catalyze the development of cutting-edge military technologies and capabilities, positioning Gulf states as self-reliant and technologically advanced defense actors on the global stage.

2. Continuous Training and Professional Development: Sustained investment in training and professional development programs is critical to cultivating a highly skilled and adaptable military workforce capable of meeting the complexities of modern warfare. Advanced training facilities equipped with sophisticated simulation technologies can replicate realistic operational scenarios and enhance the readiness and proficiency of military personnel. Moreover, fostering a culture of continuous learning through cross-training opportunities, joint exercises with allied forces, and academic partnerships can instill a mindset of agility and innovation among military personnel, enabling them to respond to dynamic security challenges effectively.

3. Seamless Coordination and Interoperability: The seamless coordination and interoperability among the armed forces of

Gulf states are essential for achieving unity of effort in joint operations and maximizing operational effectiveness. Standardizing procedures, harmonizing communication systems, and integrating command structures can streamline decision-making processes and facilitate rapid responses to emergent threats. By establishing joint training exercises, creating interoperability working groups, and leveraging digital platforms for real-time information sharing, Gulf states can enhance their ability to operate cohesively across different domains of warfare, thereby strengthening their deterrence posture and operational resilience.

4. Embrace Technological Advancements: Embracing technological advancements and fostering a culture of innovation are key enablers for enhancing military capabilities and ensuring strategic autonomy. By investing in emerging technologies such as artificial intelligence, unmanned systems, and cybersecurity solutions, Gulf states can enhance their operational effectiveness and adaptability to the evolving security landscape. Collaborating with leading technology firms, academic institutions, and defense innovation hubs can expedite the integration of cutting-edge technologies into military systems, empowering Gulf states to maintain a technological edge over potential adversaries and respond effectively to emerging threats.

5. Forge Strategic Defense Partnerships: Strategic defense partnerships with like-minded nations allow Gulf states to leverage collective expertise, resources, and interoperability in addressing shared security challenges. By strengthening alliances with key partners, Gulf states can enhance their defense capabilities, foster information sharing, and build a more robust regional security architecture. Engaging in joint military exercises, intelligence-sharing initiatives, and defense

cooperation agreements can deepen strategic relationships and contribute to a more integrated and coordinated approach to regional security challenges.
6. Enhance Intelligence and Counterterrorism Capabilities: Enhancing intelligence gathering capabilities and counterterrorism measures is essential to addressing asymmetric threats and safeguarding internal security in Gulf states. By investing in advanced intelligence collection platforms, developing comprehensive counterterrorism strategies, and fostering international collaboration in intelligence sharing, Gulf states can enhance their situational awareness and preemptive capabilities in countering terrorism and extremism. Strengthening coordination among security agencies, leveraging advanced analytical tools for threat assessment, and fortifying cybersecurity defenses can further enhance Gulf states' resilience against evolving security threats, ensuring a proactive and effective response to emerging challenges.
7. Uphold Governance and Transparency: Upholding good governance practices and transparency within the defense sector is critical for ensuring accountability, efficiency, and integrity in military operations. Establishing robust oversight mechanisms, implementing anti-corruption measures, and promoting transparency in defense procurement processes are essential steps toward building public trust and confidence in the responsible management of defense resources. Adhering to ethical standards, conducting regular audits, and fostering a culture of accountability can enhance the credibility and effectiveness of Gulf states' defense establishments, fostering greater public support and legitimacy for defense initiatives.

By integrating these comprehensive strategies and initiatives into their defense planning and policy framework, Gulf states can enhance their operational effectiveness, bolster military autonomy, and reinforce their resilience in navigating the complex and multifaceted security environment. The commitment to fostering local defense industries, investing in training and professional development, promoting seamless coordination and interoperability, embracing technological advancements, forging strategic defense partnerships, enhancing intelligence and counterterrorism capabilities, and upholding governance and transparency will position Gulf states as proactive and capable actors in advancing regional security and stability.

C. POLICY CONSIDERATIONS FOR PROMOTING NATIONAL SECURITY AND REGIONAL STABILITY

It is imperative to develop and implement strategic policies that address key challenges and opportunities facing the Gulf states to enhance national security and foster regional stability. This chapter will delve into a range of policy considerations to strengthen military capabilities, enhance cooperation, and mitigate security threats in the Gulf.

1. Diplomatic Engagement:

Diplomatic engagement plays a crucial role in shaping the security landscape of the Gulf region. Gulf states must prioritize dialogue and engagement with regional and international partners to build trust, resolve conflicts, and promote stability. Multilateral forums such as the Gulf Cooperation Council (GCC) and the Arab League provide platforms for diplomatic dialogue and collaboration on security issues. By fostering diplomatic channels and promoting dialogue, Gulf states can address regional tensions and work towards peaceful resolutions of conflicts.

2. Arms Control and Non-Proliferation:

Arms control and non-proliferation efforts are key components of regional security initiatives in the Gulf. Gulf states must adhere to international arms control agreements and strengthen export controls to prevent the spread of weapons of mass destruction. Implementing effective arms control measures, enhancing transparency in defense procurement, and promoting confidence-building measures are critical for reducing the risk of arms races and enhancing regional stability. Additionally, investing in conventional arms control agreements and cooperation on disarmament can build trust and reduce the potential for military conflicts in the Gulf region.

3. Military Modernization and Innovation:

Military modernization and innovation are essential for enhancing defense capabilities and ensuring readiness in the Gulf states. Gulf countries must invest in advanced military technologies, cybersecurity capabilities, and defense systems to address evolving security threats. Collaborating with international partners, leveraging research and development initiatives, and promoting defense innovation hubs can enhance the military effectiveness of Gulf armies and strengthen regional security. Furthermore, encouraging joint research and development projects in defense technology and fostering partnerships with academia and private industries can facilitate the adoption of cutting-edge military capabilities in the Gulf states.

4. Counterterrorism and Counterinsurgency Strategies:

The persistent threat of terrorism and insurgency poses significant challenges to the security of the Gulf region. Gulf states must develop comprehensive counterterrorism strategies that prioritize intelligence sharing, border security measures, and coordinated military operations. Enhancing cooperation among security agencies, implementing counterterrorism laws, and addressing the root causes of extremism are crucial for combating terrorism and ensuring regional stability. Moreover, investing in countering violent extremism programs, community engagement initiatives, and deradicalization efforts can help address the underlying factors contributing to terrorism in the Gulf states.

5. Defence Cooperation and Joint Exercises:

Strengthening defense cooperation and conducting joint military exercises are vital for enhancing regional security capabilities in the Gulf. Gulf states should prioritize interoperability, joint training programs, and military exercises with regional and international partners to improve readiness and response capabilities. Regular military drills, joint patrols, and information-sharing mechanisms can enhance coordination and collaboration among Gulf armies in addressing security challenges. Additionally, establishing joint defense structures, sharing intelligence resources, and coordinating crisis response mechanisms can enhance the effectiveness of defense cooperation efforts in the Gulf region.

6. *Economic Diversification and Socioeconomic Development:*

Economic diversification and socioeconomic development are key pillars of sustainable security in the Gulf states. Investing in education, healthcare, infrastructure, and job creation can address social inequalities, reduce vulnerabilities, and enhance resilience against security threats. Economic stability, job opportunities, and social welfare programs contribute to building inclusive societies and fostering long-term stability in the Gulf region. Furthermore, supporting diversification initiatives in non-oil sectors, fostering entrepreneurship and innovation, and promoting sustainable development practices can strengthen the Gulf states' economic foundations and enhance security and stability in the region.

7. *Good Governance and Rule of Law:*

Upholding principles of good governance, transparency, and the rule of law is crucial for promoting stability and security in the Gulf states. Strengthening governance structures, anti-corruption measures, and accountability mechanisms can enhance public trust, legitimacy, and support for national security initiatives. Promoting a culture of accountability, respecting human rights, and upholding the rule of law contribute to building strong institutions and fostering sustainable security in the region. Additionally, investing in judicial reform, enhancing legal frameworks, and promoting government transparency can strengthen the rule of law and promote good governance practices in the Gulf countries.

8. *Regional Security Architecture:*

A robust regional security architecture is essential for enhancing the Gulf region's cooperation, coordination, and conflict resolution mechanisms. Gulf states must engage in dialogue, multilateral security cooperation, and confidence-building measures to address common security challenges and build trust among nations. Regional security dialogues, joint security initiatives, and crisis management mechanisms can enhance collective security efforts and promote peace and stability in the Gulf region. Furthermore, fostering regional security partnerships, enhancing regional security frameworks, and promoting conflict prevention and resolution mechanisms can strengthen the regional security architecture in the Gulf states and enhance peace and stability in the region.

By adopting a comprehensive approach to national security and regional stability, Gulf states can effectively address security threats, enhance military capabilities, and promote regional cooperation. Implementing sound policy considerations is crucial for safeguarding the interests of Gulf nations and fostering a secure and prosperous future for the region.

www.ingramcontent.com/pod-product-compliance
Lightning Source LLC
Chambersburg PA
CBHW071713020426
42333CB00017B/2253